From Know-How

"Dave and Ian's approach is different and is a very effective way of stimulating you into thinking more about your own strengths and weaknesses and what you are trying to achieve."
Chris Grayling, UK Minister of Justice

"Few books on change tell you that real change comes from deeply reflective work on yourself. Even fewer books tell you how to get to that hidden inner coalface and how to dig out the coal of real change. These authors are deeply experienced practitioners and this book does. Do the reflective exercises. Your growth will come from that effort."
Jim Platts, University of Cambridge, Institute for Manufacturing

"From Know-how to Do-how explores what stops us from making changes and gets us to expose our hidden rules, often those strengths that now start to work against us. Full of practical examples and 'try this' exercises, the book shines a light on how to achieve the success of a real breakthrough that can make a difference to our lives or work."
Simon Sanders, Global Services Finance Director, Fujitsu

"This book is a must-read for all 'can do, will do' organisations. It condenses complex change theory into straightforward, effective actions."
Graham Cowley, Chief Operating Officer, Capita Symonds

"In a world where we are overwhelmed with knowledge, this book actually equips you with the insights and inspiration and more specifically the tools to turn knowledge into reality. Clarity and common sense are the hallmarks of this outstanding book."
Paul McGee, author of S.U.M.O.

From Know-How to Do-How

The short and simple guide to making change happen

Dave Corbet & Ian Roberts

NICHOLAS BREALEY
PUBLISHING

London • Boston

First published by
Nicholas Brealey Publishing in 2013

3–5 Spafield Street
Clerkenwell, London
EC1R 4QB, UK
Tel: +44 (0)20 7239 0360
Fax: +44 (0)20 7239 0370

20 Park Plaza
Boston
MA 02116, USA
Tel: (888) BREALEY
Fax: (617) 523 3708

www.nicholasbrealey.com
www.the-do-how.com

ISBN: 978-1-85788-590-3
eISBN: 978-1-85788-981-9

British Library Cataloguing in Publication Data
A catalogue record for this book is available from the British Library.

Printed in Great Britain by Clays Ltd, St Ives plc

Contents

For Dad and for Nicola

"The truth of the matter is that you always know the right thing to do. The hard part is doing it."

General Stormin' Norman Schwarzkopf

Preface

WHY WE WROTE THIS BOOK

Change doesn't have
to be complicated

A few years ago, a close friend of ours walked to the peak of a mountain called Stok Kangri. Standing at the western end of the Himalayas in Ladakh, northern India, Stok Kangri peaks at over 20,000 feet (over 6,000 meters) and is covered in snow in all but the warmest of summers. We are more familiar with walking the gentle, 3,000-feet hills of England's Lake District and were impressed at what seemed to us to be quite an achievement. "It must have been a big challenge," we suggested.

"It depends what you mean by a challenge," she said. "There was a bit of preparation, having the right gear, finding a guide, acclimatizing to the altitude, and so on, but once you get out there it's not so complicated. You just put one foot in front of the other and keep going until you reach the top."

It's the same with change. Everybody knows that change is difficult, but it doesn't have to be complicated. Some people would *prefer* change to be complicated. That way they can avoid taking responsibility for making change happen by putting it off until they have acquired yet another piece of information or developed yet another strategy. We are not saying that change is *easy*, any more than walking up a tall mountain is easy, but it's certainly *possible* if you have commitment and take the time to understand and apply a few simple principles. In this book we set out what those simple principles are. If you apply them to the challenges in your life and work, you can make a breakthrough with any change you want.

Have you ever wondered why people and organizations find it so hard to change and, more importantly, what we can do about it? More specifically, why do people sometimes get stuck in the same loops, revisiting the same commitment to change again and again but with very little actually changing? We have spent most of our working lives developing practical solutions to this problem. We have worked with over 10,000 people in hundreds of organizations helping them to make the breakthroughs they want, each time learning a little more about what is really required to make change stick. We have helped individuals and teams in government departments, local government bodies, hospitals, housing associations, and businesses from just about every sector of industry, including several FTSE 500 companies. That's where this book came from and that's where the idea of do-how came from. If know-how is about knowing what to do, do-how is about actually doing it.

INTRODUCING DO-HOW

We didn't always talk about do-how. When we first started in business nearly 20 years ago, we were like many con-

If know-how is about knowing what to do, do-how is about actually doing it

sultants. Steeped in strategic thinking, we thought that if we helped our clients figure out what they needed to do and supported them to develop the skills to do that, everything would turn out fine. But it wasn't enough. We witnessed the frustration that people felt at their lack of progress despite the undoubted commitment of all involved to the agreed changes. We saw at first hand how the very best of intentions were diverted off course time and again, as if some invisible force were guiding events. We met teams where everyone knew what they needed to do, but that know-how wasn't enough actually to bring about much-needed change. There's a very big difference between know-how and do-how – and in that difference lies the key to successful change.

Once we realized this, our work took a new direction. We became fascinated by the psychology of change in both teams and individuals. We read everything we could get our hands on and visited whoever would talk to us about change. We distilled lessons from NLP and psychology and recombined them with insights drawn from disciplines as diverse as spiral dynamics, narrative therapy, and appreciative inquiry. We studied what those with a proven track record of bringing about change had to say: people like Marshall Goldsmith, Jim Loehr, Werner Erhard, John Grinder, Thich Nhat Hanh, and John Kotter. But most of all, we practiced. Through hard graft and the determination to deliver for our clients the breakthroughs they so badly wanted, we learned what worked and what really helped people and organizations to change. What we learned is that there are a small number of simple steps that, if applied with rigor and discipline, lead to a breakthrough. These steps aren't difficult to understand or even to apply. The issue is simply that many people get lost in the confusion, give up after the first setback, or lack the discipline and self-belief to see change through. This is true in both life and work.

And that is why we wrote this book. Our clients told us that what we were doing was different, and that it helped them find a way forward where they had struggled before. We, too, could see this in the results we were getting. Teams that had been stuck, in some cases for years, unable to make the changes they wanted, suddenly made a breakthrough. People whose careers had stalled found themselves on a new, upward trajectory. And the approaches were not merely applicable to work. Some clients told us that they had used the ideas we teach in this book to make significant breakthroughs at home. We had found a practical and reliable way to help any individual, any team, or any organization make the changes they wanted and to make those changes stick.

This might seem like a bold claim, but we can say this because we have abundant evidence that these methods work. What we describe in these pages is simply what we do with our clients and they tell us time and again that what we recommend works, often where other practices have stalled or failed. Here are a few of the things our clients have said when we've asked them for feedback about the techniques we use:

"Makes what seems impossible, practical and achievable."

"I have immediately been able to make a breakthrough on a long-term problem."

"Will have a potentially massive impact on the way I will work."

"Had an immediate impact – challenged some of my management practices which I have since changed."

"Has helped us to make more progress in the last six months than we achieved in the last six years."

"Made an impact immediately – used the techniques in meetings with staff in the week following the course and have made a breakthrough in my personal performance."

"I could have done with this five years ago. The best training course I've ever been on."

"Much better than other training I have attended as it actually provides practical ways for improving performance."

WHAT'S THE DIFFERENCE?

So what is so different about our approach that it delivers such great results? The answer is what we call the "do-how map," which brings together diverse aspects of change in one simple, yet thoroughly practical, tried-and-tested model. The do-how map helps anyone navigate the changes they want to make and cuts through the overwhelming fog of complexity, which can be one of the greatest barriers to change. Furthermore, the area our clients most regularly highlight as a uniquely powerful aspect of our methods is our emphasis on using negative emotions as a pointer to opportunities to make a breakthrough. The role of negative emotions in change is often overlooked or even deliberately avoided. Yet in our experience, this aspect of change, while challenging, is ultimately highly rewarding and leads to the most significant breakthroughs.

In the first three chapters of this book we discuss the challenges of making change happen. We explore what really gets in the way and we introduce the do-how map. Chapters 4 to 7 expand the four main branches of the do-how map and illustrate how these have helped people make significant breakthroughs. The final three chapters explain how to apply the do-how map to both organizational and personal change.

Some of what we say will challenge you. On the other hand, some of the book may appear to be too simple to make much of an impact or seem so obvious that it doesn't need stating. We make no apologies for this. In our experience it is often the fact that people have lost sight of the easy things they can do that leads to them feeling stuck. Other parts of what we say might appear to be contrary to common sense at first reading. In particular, we make some statements about people in general that you may feel are too sweeping and certainly don't apply to you. However, we want to emphasize that this is not a theoretical book. Everything we describe is based on real breakthroughs with our clients, and on what we have observed through our own direct experience. All of the examples and case studies are based on real people and real situations; while most are drawn from business, the essential lessons apply in both life and work. The names and some of the details have been changed to protect the anonymity of the people mentioned.

What has worked for the people and teams we have worked with can work for you. If you take the time to understand and apply what we have to share in this book, you will possess the tools you need to make any breakthrough you set your mind to. However, developing do-how can't be done by reading a book, even this book. Do-how comes from altering the way you look at the world and changing your behavior. To get the most out of this book, we very much hope that you will complete the exercises as you go along. The techniques and exercises we describe are those we use with our clients. They are intended to give you insights into your own assumptions and ways of looking at things. The exercises build on each other to give you a unique understanding of how you think, how this thinking limits you, and how you can make your own breakthrough, whether in life or work. In this way you will be able to test the validity of what we are saying for yourself and develop the do-how you need to make the breakthrough you want.

You can make a breakthrough

Some of the exercises require you to make notes or do a little writing, so before going any further, get yourself a pen and a notebook so that you are ready for action – ready to really learn about yourself, to move from know-how to do-how.

Chapter 1

DO YOU HAVE THE DO-HOW?

What do-how is and
why it matters

There is an old story from Russia about a peasant farmer who got his handcart stuck in the mud on the way to market. He heaved away at the cart, but nothing he tried would move it forward. Although the farmer was strong, the harder he pushed the deeper the cart got stuck. He was becoming more and more distressed by the situation and even started kicking the cart and cursing the mud. "My cart is stuck and I can't get it moving again. All my produce for the market will be ruined and I won't be able to buy food for my family," he wailed.

A young man, seeing the farmer's distress, offered to help. He could immediately spot what the problem was. The more the farmer pushed, the more the mud was building up under the wheels. The cart would have to be pulled backward before it could go forward. "Have you tried pulling the cart back out of the mud instead of pushing it?" the young man asked. "Let me see if I can help you move it."

"It's no use," said the farmer, "I've tried everything and it won't budge forward an inch. I've pulled from the front; I've pushed from the back. If only the authorities would repair this track. If only it didn't rain so much. If only the market weren't so far away. There's nothing more I can do!" he bellowed.

Despite these protestations, the young man grabbed the handle and started pulling the cart backward. He wasn't as strong as the farmer and could hardly move the cart but, inch by inch, he started to drag it out of the mud. The farmer suddenly saw what the young man was trying to do and joined him in pulling the cart backward out of the mud. After a few minutes it had successfully returned to the hard stones of the track. The joyful farmer thanked the young man for this miracle, as he saw it, and went on his way, diverting the cart around the deeper mud.

This story illustrates what we mean by do-how. Moving forward seems impossible to the farmer. He feels like he has tried everything. Even when the young man suggests an alternative course of action, the farmer doesn't try it because he can't imagine that it will work. More know-how or expertise isn't going to help. He is trapped, not only by the mud, but by his own way of thinking about the problem. It is only when he witnesses what the young man is doing that he can see the sense in it. The young man not only has the know-how needed to move the cart, he has the do-how. By taking what he knows and putting it into action, he demonstrates a new way of thinking and acting in relation to the situation and the farmer's problem is quickly solved.

This is do-how – the ability to translate know-how into action consistent with what you want to achieve. If know-how is *knowing what to do* to get what you want, do-how is *doing what needs to be done* to get what you want. There's a big difference.

> **Do-how = the ability to translate know-how into action consistent with what you want to achieve**

KNOW-HOW ISN'T ENOUGH

We spend our time working with individuals, teams, and businesses that want to make a breakthrough. The people we work with are smart, successful, and ambitious. They have a lot of expertise and know-how and possess the commitment they need to drive change. What stands out is just how many people have felt like the farmer in our story. They are frustrated by the slow pace of change. Whether we are dealing with personal change or large-scale, organization-wide change, progress is difficult.

However, what also stands out is quite how quickly things can move once people see what the problem is. And the problem with change is rarely a lack of know-how. The bookshelves are groaning with the weight of the world's expertise on every imaginable aspect of personal development and organizational change. In business, most of the people we come across have had all the management and leadership training they can bear and know almost everything they need to do a great job. Further training usually results in the accusation of "teaching grandmother to suck eggs." And yet still they feel frustrated in their efforts to make change happen.

We often encounter people who can happily tell us all about the nuances of performance management or goal setting or whatever other skill is needed to bring about change, although that rarely means that they put all that learning into practice. For example, in our development programs our request that participants write down their goals rarely meets with great enthusiasm. They already know about goals, so they wonder why they need to bother. We persevere and after a brief discussion of the basics of effective goal setting, we review their goals.

Our experience is that less than 20 percent of people in the room will have well-defined, positive goals. And that's the key point. Most of what we need to learn to be good at leading people and driving change isn't difficult to understand. It's easy for people to learn the techniques and the theory. People usually have all the know-how they require, but they less often put it into practice with consistency and commitment. We are sure that you have met many people who are convinced that they are good listeners, who have all the techniques to hand, yet somehow they can't keep quiet and listen. Or perhaps you have suffered from a manager who has learned all about delegation but in reality fails to delegate.

HABITS, CULTURE, AND CHOICE

The problem in making change happen isn't learning new knowledge or skills. It's realizing that we already have preferred, habitual patterns of thinking and behaving that are largely invisible to us, and that we can't adopt new ways of working unless we are ready to let go of the existing ways. It's only when people are willing to relinquish their old ways of thinking and start behaving in a way that is consistent with the outcomes they want to achieve that change can take root and blossom. That is why the farmer in our story is stuck. Even when the way forward is pointed out to him, he can't see it because his habitual behavior is to push hard in the direction he wants to go; that simply isn't going to work in this situation. He doesn't even realize that he's making a choice about his behavior. To his mind he has tried everything.

Everyone has habitual ways of thinking and behaving and every organization has cultural norms that determine acceptable behavior in that organization. Those habits guide the choices we make about how to behave. We have met many effective people who have habits that have helped them accomplish great things. Whatever the source of their success is, it becomes habitual for them to behave that way. For example, the more attention we pay to building relationships, the more we develop the skills required and the less conscious thought we need to access those skills. The more decisive we are, the easier it becomes to be decisive.

Habits help us to navigate the complexity of the world around us. Without them we would struggle to make all the choices we are confronted with even in a single day. And our habitual choices occur without the need for conscious thought; in fact, we stop noticing that any choice is being made at all. In this way our habits place boundaries on the range of behaviors we are likely to adopt. We don't notice that we think and behave in limited ways because our thinking and behavior are so familiar. None of this is a problem – until we need to change.

When behaviors that have served us well no longer fit the circumstances we are in, or when the demands of the organization confront us with the need to change, that is when we feel stuck. And that is when all the know-how in the world can't help us. We need the breakthrough from know-how to do-how. For example, people who are successful largely because of their ability to listen may stumble when confronted with circumstances that require swift and decisive action. On the other hand, those whose success is built on their decisiveness often struggle with situations in which they need to slow down and nurture support from other parts of the business. In a successful career this kind of challenge, far from being a rarity, is almost the norm.

It is the same for organizations. In every business we have ever worked with, the staff exhibited some common patterns of acceptable thinking and behavior, which we usually call the corporate culture. The culture of the organization tells everyone who works there what is important and what actions will lead to success. For example, we have experienced organizations where there seems to be an unwritten rule that no one should ever take any risks, no matter how small; we have worked in other companies where the unwritten rule seems to be always to move into action as quickly as possible. People who don't like the culture tend to leave or adjust their own behavior to fit in with what the organization seems to want from them.

The way people in any company think and behave seems normal to those who have become accustomed to the way that organization works. To anyone who has worked there for a long time, what started as an unwritten rule becomes a hidden rule: "It's just the way we do things around here." Culture develops in response to the needs of the business at that time and underpins its success. It limits the range of acceptable behaviors and is effectively invisible. Again, that's not a problem – until the organization needs to change.

Faced with such a requirement, senior executives may meet to agree their strategy and possibly even implement an organizational change program to underpin the direction they want to take the business in. However, they are likely to find that something keeps getting in the way of change happening. That something is the culture, which will smother change unless new ways of working consistent with where the company is heading are explicitly brought to life. It is not enough, for example, simply to state that the company needs to be less risk averse or that managers need to devolve decision making. These ideas have to be transformed into *action*. That is what we mean by do-how.

Many organizational change programs fail because they focus on structures and systems and processes, without taking culture into account. They fail because the structures, the systems, and the processes are a reflection of the present culture and altering them won't lead to fundamental change. Most often when a company is struggling, the problem is not in the structures or the IT system, it is in people's behavior and ways of thinking. Change those and everything else will follow. The more senior and influential a person is, the more important is the way they think and behave and the more impact they have on the organization as a whole. Unless people understand what behaviors and ways of thinking are consistent with where the business is going rather than where it has come from, then nothing in fact changes. Developing this kind of organizational do-how is what drives change and leads to the breakthrough in performance that organizations seek.

We have worked with organizations that have restructured their workforce again and again, yet still nothing changes. People may sit in different places on the organizational chart, but they are still the same people working in the same way and getting largely the same results. That is why so many organizational change programs really do feel like *déjà vu*, as any lasting change is neutralized by the existing culture and the next generation of senior managers faces the same challenges again a few years down the road.

DO-HOW MAKES THE DIFFERENCE

Change happens when we learn to turn our know-how into do-how. This is true whether we are talking about organizational change or individual change; whether you want to transform the way your business works or make a breakthrough in your personal life. Do-how is what makes the difference.

When someone who claims to know all about goal setting stops and takes the time to communicate a razor-sharp goal, or when a manager who has learned about delegation confronts his or her own discomfort and actually delegates, that is when change happens. Making that kind of choice is the real breakthrough. That is what changes people and that is what ultimately changes organizations. It is the same with personal development. Whether you want to make a breakthrough in your career or build better relationships at home, changes in what you do count for so much more than changes in what you know.

There are a huge range of circumstances in which do-how makes a difference and we will give lots of examples throughout the book, but we want to offer you a few to whet your appetite and illustrate what do-how can do for you.

REIGNITE YOUR CAREER

Teri was a branch manager for a mobile phone retailer. When we first met her on one of our training programs, she related a story about how intimidated she had felt by an angry customer who came to the store one day. The man was angry because his application for credit had been turned down and he couldn't get the phone deal he wanted. Teri said that despite attending numerous training programs on dealing with difficult people and handling conflict, there was nothing she could do to calm him down. We asked her what she had tried.

Teri: I tried everything! I told him that the decision had been taken by our credit control team at head office and that I could do nothing about it. I explained that the rules and regulations covering credit applications had been applied rigorously and that the considered opinion of the credit control team was that this application would breach the requirements and I showed him how he could check his own credit rating himself. I tried to talk through the best deal he could get without credit, but he didn't want to listen.

Ian: Did you try listening to his concerns?

Teri: I told him I understood his concerns.

Ian: What were his concerns?

Teri: I'm not sure.

In other words, Teri had not listened to or understood why the man was angry. How did the customer feel he had been treated? Did he think the system was unfair? Perhaps he had a grudge against the company? Teri had told the man all kinds of facts and opinions of her own, but had not tested any of the techniques that would be taught on any basic program about dealing with conflict. She had tried one approach in various shades and tones and at increasing volume and had failed to see that there was no real variation in her behavior. She had played the situation like a right-handed tennis player who can only play forehand and looks on bemused every time a ball passes on her left. Any problem that required a variation on offering up facts or opinions left her puzzled and more than a little stressed. It was not that she lacked the skills or knowledge; it was just that in the heat of this difficult situation all she could do was revert to her favored behavior, giving people answers.

Teri's problem was not a lack of know-how. She had been on the right courses and could recite the basics of conflict resolution and customer care. Her problem was simply a lack of ability to choose a response that would have been more appropriate to the person she was faced with. She had been unaware of this and therefore had no real choice in her behavior. The problem was not know-how; it was do-how. Coming to this realization was a huge breakthrough for her. Following this insight, and with very little further support, her career took off as she showed herself capable of dealing with the trickiest situations.

MAKE A BREAKTHROUGH AT WORK

Do you ever feel stuck like the farmer described at the start of this chapter? Change is difficult at the best of times, but sometimes it can seem impossible to make progress. We want to reassure you that whatever breakthrough you are looking for, change *is* possible. Just like the young man in the story, you can find a new approach or a way of looking at things that will allow you to move forward.

Our clients have made all kinds of breakthroughs using the methods we help them learn. These range from attracting a multimillion investment in a company that had been starved of investment for decades through to reinvigorating a team's commitment to a shared set of goals. We are sure that you will recognize some of the more common challenges we have helped clients with. These include:

➠ Gaining buy-in to a significant change
➠ Building a shared vision and a commitment to delivering it
➠ Dealing with underperforming team members
➠ Generating trust within a team and across different teams or organizations
➠ Handling a difficult relationship with a new boss

⇒ Holding people to account for what they have promised they will deliver
⇒ Finding time for strategic thinking when the day is full of urgent challenges
⇒ Coping with having too many things to do with too few resources
⇒ Learning to say no
⇒ Transforming a fear of giving presentations
⇒ Raising difficult issues without causing offense
⇒ Recruiting leaders rather than followers
⇒ Finding an opportunity when there only seem to be problems

Alan had risen to be the chief executive of a very large contract catering company with 20,000 employees in hundreds of locations. All through his career he had frequently been praised for his intelligence, particularly his highly developed capacity to see all sides of an argument and find a compromise. He had been promoted rapidly and at the age of 43 found himself at the peak of his career. Then the tide had turned. His senior team was in conflict, with individual departments taking their own course and no coherent strategy for the business as a whole. He found himself surrounded by criticism and talk of weak leadership.

What was the problem? Did Alan lack the skills to develop an effective strategy for the organization? Was it that he didn't have the communication and influencing skills to take his fellow directors with him? Far from it, he had all these qualities. The problem was that he lacked the ability to choose a way of thinking and behaving that was appropriate for this challenging situation. He had always been admired for his ability to see all sides of an argument. This had worked well when he had someone above him making the really tough decisions that any complex organization faces. Now he was in the driving seat, the organization faced some difficult decisions, and his lack of behavioral flexibility was getting in the way. He lacked the do-how.

"People don't understand how incredibly complex the organization is," he explained. "These aren't decisions to be taken lightly. We need a strategy that has something in it for everyone. I'm taking the time to understand the concerns of all sides and see how they fit together." In other words, he was doing everything but making the hard choices the organization needed. While he was finessing and polishing his ideas, he never seemed to get to the point where he actually pinned his colors to the mast and declared the way forward. He was savvy enough to realize that he needed a breakthrough and he sought help from us.

What made the difference for Alan was when his habit of trying to come up with the perfect answer, something that had been suggested by various coaches and even by members of his team, was confirmed by his wife, the one person whose judgment he really trusted and whose feedback he would take seriously. He realized that his deputy, whom he had rubbed up against in the past because of his "bullish nature," was just the person he needed by his side and he started to listen to the deputy's advice more when it came to tough decisions. Alan's motto became: "A good plan today is better than a great plan tomorrow." It was a huge step forward and he avoided a career-ending failure.

MAKE A BREAKTHROUGH AT HOME

The main thrust of this book is to help you make the changes you want at work, but much of what we discuss is equally applicable to your personal life. Indeed, many of our clients have shared with us how our approaches have helped them with all kinds of personal goals and challenges in bringing about the changes they want at home as well as in business. One client used the idea of do-how to carve a whole hour off his personal best for the Ironman Triathlon and competed at a national level. Another made a breakthrough with his teenage son after several years of an increasingly difficult relationship.

This should not be too surprising, since what we talk about in this book is how people make breakthroughs. It doesn't matter whether we are considering work or personal life, the same principles apply and the same techniques can work. Some of the ways our clients have used our approaches in their personal lives include:

- Improving performance at sporting activities
- Improving relationships with partners and children, especially teenage children

⮕ Dealing with unsatisfactory service from tradespeople or retailers
⮕ Completing major household projects such as building an extension
⮕ Making a major decision such as changing job or moving house

DEVELOP YOUR ORGANIZATION

Most of our work is with large businesses and there is nothing more difficult to change than the culture of a large organization. Nevertheless, the approaches we outline in this book have produced change where many other approaches have stalled.

We worked with a water company to help create a breakthrough in the way it worked. The managing director, Geoff, had recently been appointed to the position and wanted to create a faster-paced culture focused on innovation and performance. He knew that he had his work cut out. The company had a history of failed change programs and many staff were skeptical that real change was possible. The organization was very slow moving and relied heavily on bureaucratic processes.

One of the most dominant aspects of the existing culture was a strong hierarchy and a reliance on prescriptive and complex procedures to drive out all risk. This had risen out of a need to ensure compliance with the industry's rigorous quality standards, but reached into every aspect of the business. A consequence of this culture was that anyone on the front line of the organization who came across a problem would pass it up to their boss for a decision on what to do. The boss would then pass it on to their boss, and so on all the way up. Decision making was grindingly slow and that was why the company was being left behind by nimbler competitors. This long-standing culture made it very reliable, but also meant that changes took too long. Many of the procedures had become "tick-box" exercises with little attention given to the real purpose behind them, as managers had grown used to the idea that someone more senior would take ultimate responsibility for any decisions.

Geoff recognized that change was required and implemented a range of programs, including restructuring from five divisions down to three and investing heavily in improved IT systems. He also knew that the current culture was slowing down progress and asked us to work with him to implement his vision for how the company could work.

The whole senior team had bought into a vision of a faster-moving company with less bureaucracy and more responsibility for decisions delegated to the discretion of individual managers. Geoff called this a culture of asking for forgiveness rather than permission. Senior executives could easily grasp what it meant to give their staff the authority to make decisions and choices about how to respond to day-to-day challenges. They had the know-how; the challenge came when they were faced with aligning their own behavior with that vision.

One of the biggest champions of the changes was the head of human resources, Jill, a bright and energetic woman in her mid-30s. She had joined the company six years earlier and expressed frustration at the bureaucratic culture. She had taken on the task of overhauling the performance appraisal system. At a meeting with the senior management team, Jill presented a one-page guidance note on performance management. The document essentially said that each manager must provide protected time for a one-to-one discussion about performance with each of their direct reports at least once a month, and must also agree performance development goals with each direct report at least once a year. This was intended to replace a long-winded and highly prescriptive document that set out precisely what a manager must do to review performance, together with various tables and forms to fill out. The new note was very much in line with the vision, in that it gave guidance rather than instructions and left much of the detail to the discretion of the individual line manager.

While a few of the senior team loved what Jill had presented, the reaction of some of the other senior managers was a mixture of bewilderment and horror. "What if they get it wrong?" was one reaction. "Shouldn't we agree the best way to conduct a one-to-one meeting?" was another. What they were experiencing was what we call a *do-how moment*. What they chose to do in this moment would either reinforce the old culture or demonstrate the new culture they were trying to create.

They loved the idea of managers "taking responsibility for making decisions," but they didn't reckon on how strong their reaction would be to the changes in their own behavior that this required. The problem was that they had habitually taken decisions on behalf of staff. By working through the steps we describe later in this book, they spotted the consequences of old ways of thinking and behaving and how these underpinned the organization's present culture. They were able to confront their anxieties about choosing to let go of their old habits. That is when they made the breakthrough from know-how to do-how. As a result, the culture started to shift and the company began its journey to become recognized as an industry leader.

WHEN DO WE NEED DO-HOW?

Understanding do-how can transform a whole range of situations, but there are four factors that seem to arise again and again that characterize when do-how can be a particularly powerful tool:

➠ **When making a breakthrough really matters.** When the stakes are really high and if you don't make a breakthrough then something is going to break down or fail, that's when you need do-how.

➠ **When you feel stuck.** Whatever you try, you feel like you're going around in circles, having the same conversations and returning to the same old problems. You feel like you have tried everything and doing what you normally do just isn't getting you anywhere. Phrases like "I've tried it all before" or "Nothing ever changes around here" or "Why does it always happen to me?" are dead giveaways that you need more do-how.

➠ **When playing to your strengths is not enough.** Understanding what you are good at is important. But sometimes, the mantra of positive psychology "play to your strengths" simply isn't enough. When the very strengths that brought you success are holding you back, it's time to let go and try another stroke. It is important to realize that you can choose your behavior rather than allowing your behavior to choose you. That is the real point of self-awareness, knowing that you are making choices and what those choices are. Your real strengths are the ones you can let go of when you need to.

➦ **When emotions are negative**. When you are unhappy with your lot but seem to lack the ability to do anything but complain, or if you notice that you are regularly angry or frustrated or saddened by the situations you find yourself in, it's time for some do-how.

Teri spoke to us about her frustration at being passed over for yet another promotion. She could see her career stalling and this mattered to her. She felt like she was stuck, sent on yet another unnecessary training course that wouldn't make any difference because she knew all she needed to know about customer service and communication skills. She had bumped up against the limits of her strengths and she needed to find a new way forward.

Alan was a man in crisis. The stakes couldn't have been higher for him or for his business. Yet he knew that the strengths that had delivered for him in the past were not providing the breakthrough he needed. He was going around in circles and facing personal disaster.

Geoff could see that the organization was stuck, going around the same loop, coming up with a well-meaning mission statement that changed nothing and only reinforced the feeling of "nothing ever changes around here." The organization's main strength, its ability to drive out all risk, was now limiting its ability to adapt and thrive.

Do-how is what made the difference in all of these examples.

DO YOU HAVE THE DO-HOW?

Whatever change we want to make, the real question we need to ask is not "Do I have the know-how?" but "Do I have the do-how?" The challenge is to develop the capacity to translate our know-how into action that is consistent with what we want to achieve. It is not enough, for example, to *want* to be a good listener or to devolve decision making.

Even if we have been on all the right training programs and know the tools and techniques that can help us to do these things, we actually need to stop and listen, or have the courage to let someone else take a decision.

Of course, knowing what to do isn't the same as actually doing it. And what is more, to make a breakthrough you have to be able to choose your response in the heat of your emotional reaction to a challenging situation. It is in that moment of choice, when you act in line with what you are committed to achieving rather than out of habit, that the real breakthrough is made.

But how do you develop the freedom to let go of habitual patterns of thinking and behavior and translate your know-how into action aligned with the breakthrough you want? To do this you need to know more about your habitual behavior and the ways in which it limits your choices.

TRY THIS: WHAT CHANGE DO YOU WANT TO MAKE?
Write a list of the areas where you feel stuck or you want to make a breakthrough. Think about areas of your work or life where you feel it's difficult to make progress, where you are frustrated with the pace of change, or where you want a different result than the one you are getting now. If you have goals, write these down too. Focus on two or three breakthroughs that would make a significant impact in your work or life.

This information will be used as the raw material against which you can test the ideas in this book.

Chapter 2

THE HIDDEN RULES OF
SUCCESS (AND FAILURE)
How small changes lead
to big breakthroughs

D id you ever see the film *Groundhog Day*? A self-centered and manipulative weather reporter called Phil, played by Bill Murray, is sent to cover the annual Groundhog Day festivities at a small town called Punxsutawney. He has finished his report, but a blizzard prevents him from returning home. He wakes in his hotel room the next morning and is bewildered to find that he is living the previous day all over again. The same happens the next morning, and the next. He soon realizes that he is living the same Groundhog Day over and over again. At first his preferred pastime is to try to seduce women, including his fellow reporter Rita, played by Andie MacDowell. Every day he tries a new way to impress her or manipulate her to get her into bed. He fails miserably each time and eventually he loses hope and attempts by various means to end his life, only to awake the next morning to the same routine.

A chance remark from Rita opens Phil up to the potential of his situation and he becomes obsessed with saving the life of an old, homeless man whom he sees die in the cold weather. He learns about medicine and starts to spot opportunities to help other people. As he himself develops, he becomes less concerned about his own needs and desires and spends his time crafting ways to intervene in other people's lives and make them happy. Eventually, Rita sees the attraction of this selfless new man and that night they fall asleep in each other's arms. The following morning they find that the cycle has been broken and it is the day after Groundhog Day.

You may not be stuck in a time loop, living the same events over again, but it is easy to underestimate the extent to which your habitual ways of thinking and behaving create your situation. Because of your habits, you will inevitably find yourself in the same kind of predicament again and again. The way you think has a huge impact on the way you behave and therefore on what you achieve. The truth is that, whatever challenges or good fortune you meet, these flow at least as much from your current way of thinking and behaving as from the vagaries of circumstances that are beyond your control.

Andy is a friend of ours who likes to travel. As a young man he would set off at any opportunity with nothing but a backpack, his passport, and a winning smile. Whenever he returned from one of his hitch-hiking tours, he would tell stories of friendly people who invited him into their homes or offered him the use of their car. When asked why such good fortune seemed to happen to him so frequently, his reply was that the people he met were simply friendly. Those who knew him well thought it was more likely that Andy saw everyone as friendly and so treated the people he came across like long-lost friends. He noticed other people's friendliness, but didn't realize that the roots of this lay in his own positive attitude toward them. This feature helped him rise to become a partner in one of the largest industrial design firms in the United States.

On the other hand, Neil had recently been released from his position as a trainee barrister when we met him. His boss had complained that he was too argumentative. "Were you?" we asked. "No! It was everyone else in the company!" he complained angrily. We tried to talk the problem through with him, but soon found ourselves embroiled in a heated discussion, Neil challenging every point we made. Ironically, he had been attracted to the legal profession because he saw it as an outlet for the sharpness and precision of his mind, but these same strengths meant that he tended to get into debate with everyone he came into contact with. He noticed the arguments, but had never realized that their roots lay within his own need to win every point. He was stuck because his sharpness of mind, clearly a strength for a barrister, was the only shot in his locker. His failure to let go of his highly developed hunger to win arguments created endless drama around him and nearly cost him his career.

The challenges we face flow from our current way of thinking and behaving

We can see the same patterns at play in teams and organizations. Whatever the challenge, whether a company overburdened by bureaucracy or people failing to communicate or a lack of creativity and innovation, you can be pretty certain that the roots of the problem lie in the way that people habitually think and behave.

Whatever change you want to create in your life or your business, you would do well to start by looking in the mirror. For example, if an organization's senior managers are dissatisfied with the lack of creativity shown by staff and want to do something that will really make a difference, a good place to begin would be to look at how their own ways of thinking and behaving have previously stifled creativity and

Even small changes in the way you think and behave can lead to a breakthrough

the changes they now need to make in their own behavior to release their staff's creativity. When we have the courage to acknowledge the part our own ways of thinking and behaving play in creating and sustaining the problems we want to solve, that's when we start the journey from know-how to do-how. If we can do that, there is always the possibility of change.

THE RULES OF SUCCESS

Even small changes in the way you think and behave can lead to a breakthrough. To understand how this happens, it is useful to examine in more detail how our thoughts and behavior interact with our circumstances.

There is a model that shows how the results we get are related to the reality we face and our response to that reality. We call this the three Rs. Like the traditional three Rs in school (reading, 'riting, and 'rithmetic), the three Rs are very simple but also foundational. If we can master them we can find the best way forward with any problem or opportunity. The three Rs look like this:

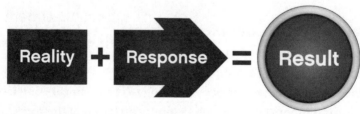

Figure 1 The three Rs

This model is used in many different fields, including strategy, consulting, leadership, coaching, cognitive therapy, and personal development. There are many ways to describe each part, as in Figure 2:

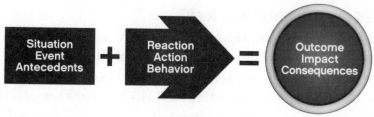

Figure 2   Other ways of describing the three Rs

For example, suppose that your reality is that someone has criticized some of your work that you thought was perfectly okay. How you respond to that reality will determine the results you get. You can say nothing, or you can find out more about why he criticized you, or you might even get angry. Each of these will lead to a different outcome. If you say nothing, your colleague might think that you agree with his comments. If you ask why he criticized your work, you might get some valuable feedback. If you become angry, he might decide to keep quiet in the future and you won't learn much.

Of course, this model provides only a snapshot of an ongoing process. Each result feeds back into the reality to form a new reality, and our response to that provides a new result, and so on. Whether you are getting what you want or are unhappy with the way things are, the model describes what is happening. Although you may not be conscious of it, your actions or behavior combine with an event or situation and determine the result or outcome. This is true for both individuals and organizations.

So for any reality there are some ways of responding that are more likely to get you the result you want. The task is to find the best course of action. Of course, this depends on precisely the result you want and how you see reality. The three Rs give us three simple rules that we can follow to ensure that we are successful:

Decide what **results** you want

Understand your **reality**

Choose the **response** most likely to get the result you want given your reality

27

DECIDE WHAT **RESULTS** YOU WANT

Whatever challenge you face or change you want to make, the best starting point is to decide the results you want. In other words, how would you like things to turn out? Every human being has the capacity to consciously decide the result they want given the circumstances they face. We call this the *capacity of intention.*

In the example above, you would need to be clear about what your intention was before you could decide how to respond. Do you simply want to defend your work or do you want to learn from the criticism? Or maybe it is more important that you build a good, ongoing relationship with your colleague. These goals all lead to potentially different actions.

Being clear about your intentions or goals has a profound impact on what you achieve. When you make a commitment to create a given outcome, you can focus your energy and attention on delivering it. Your actions become more proactive and less reactive and you are far more likely to have an impact. By being clear and explicit about the results you want, you can identify what you need to do to make a breakthrough.

Yet in our experience few people are clear about what they want. In fact, many people find it easier to say what they *don't* want, and are driven more by avoiding this than by any desire to create a specific, positive outcome. Even in organizations where there is a clear vision, many individuals will be less clear about their personal goals or those for their team.

UNDERSTAND YOUR **REALITY**

Understanding your situation can be very important in choosing the best way forward. How can you decide which direction to take if you don't know where you are? Returning to the previous example, in order to figure out what to do next it would help to know why your colleague criticized you. Was it because he had misunderstood what you had done? Or was it because he genuinely thought you hadn't done a good job? Could he have a grudge against you because of something else that has happened? Until you know the facts, it is difficult to see the way forward.

The extent to which you see what is there to be seen and the way you interpret what you see have a big impact on your choices and therefore on the results you get. You develop this understanding through your *capacity for awareness*. Awareness is like a searchlight shining on reality. The brighter and clearer it is, the more of reality you see. If your awareness of what is going on is limited or distorted, you restrict the possible choices that you think are available for action. If you only see part of the picture, you might feel that there is nothing you can do. If you have mistaken views about what the situation is, or do not have sufficient evidence at your disposal, you cannot make good choices about which actions will have the most impact.

By broadening your understanding of reality and examining the hidden assumptions in the way you look at things, you can make a breakthrough. For example, whether you focus your awareness on your own feelings about your colleague's criticism, on his reasons for criticizing you, or what you need to do differently next time will lead to a very different view of the reality of the situation and possibly a different course of action.

CHOOSE THE **RESPONSE** MOST LIKELY TO GET THE RESULTS YOU WANT GIVEN YOUR REALITY

It is fairly obvious that if you face the same situation and choose a different response, you will get a different result. This is where know-how helps, because if you have an understanding of what works you can select the approach most likely to help. For example, if you have had some training in receiving feedback, you might know the best way to handle critical comments.

Of course, that know-how is only of value if you do indeed *choose* your response. Although this is very obvious, it is extraordinary how many people act repeatedly in a way that doesn't get them the outcome they want. They then moan that the world doesn't treat them fairly or that there was nothing else they could have done. If you get angry at your colleague for criticizing you, is that because it is the best course of action (perhaps he is very negative minded and you want to point that out) or is it because you are in the habit of getting angry? Are you choosing your response or is your response choosing you?

THREE RULES FOR SUCCESS:
- **Decide what results you want**
- **Understand your reality**
- **Choose the response most likely to get the result you want given your reality**

Everyone has the ability to use these three rules and find the best way forward in any situation. By consistently and determinedly using them we can make the changes we want so that what is possible for us is limited only by our imagination, not our circumstances.

HIDDEN RULES

If making a breakthrough really is as straightforward as following three simple rules, you might be wondering why most people don't get the results they want every time. The problem is that we don't follow the three Rs because we have our own, hidden rules that prevent us from doing what we need to do. These rules are in the form of thoughts, which are so familiar that we have stopped noticing them and thus they become hidden – thoughts such as "I must always win the argument" or "I must avoid any form of conflict." It is these thoughts or hidden rules that drive our habitual behavior.

Do you remember that little paperclip on older versions of Microsoft Word, the one that always thought it knew what you were trying to do? It would pop up and dance around making suggestions when you tried to do something that it thought it recognized: "It looks like you are writing a letter, would you like help with that?" It was almost universally disliked, as it often misinterpreted what you were doing. It had a set of rules that told it when to pop up, but they didn't quite work. Our hidden rules are just like that paperclip.

We all play the game of life by hidden rules. These rules tell you what is good or bad, right or wrong, true or untrue, possible or impossible. They define the boundaries of your behavior, telling you what you must do and what you mustn't do. They show you what to focus on and what to ignore. Your hidden rules determine what goals you set, what you notice about reality, and how you respond to any given situation. Because they are hidden, you don't realize that you are making choices about your behavior or when those choices are in conflict with the three Rs.

The world is just too complex for you consciously to experience and respond to everything. Your senses provide information at a rate faster than the fastest broadband, yet you can only handle a very small proportion of what you perceive. Your hidden rules filter how you process all that raw sensory data and attach meaning to it. They help you to make sense of the world and decide how to react, otherwise you would just melt down in all the complexity. But like Clippy the paperclip, they also pop up when you encounter what seems to be a familiar situation.

We play the game of life by hidden rules

WHO CHOOSES YOUR BEHAVIOR?

You don't notice your hidden rules and because you don't notice them they limit the choices of what you think, say, and do. If you don't know that you are limiting your choice of behavior, then you don't have the freedom to choose.

For example, it is easy to see that "I must never upset people" is merely an idea. It is a useful thought in some circumstances but limiting in others. However, to the person who has that thought habitually, it takes on the status of a rule or a universal law that must never be broken. This person will be very easy-going and probably likeable, but will get stuck when she comes up against a situation where the only way forward is for someone to be upset.

You may consider that you have the freedom to think and behave in any way you want and that you don't have any rules governing how you act. That may be the case but if so, you are a rare individual indeed and you don't need the help we offer in this book.

We were discussing these ideas with Raj, a long-time client and friend. By his own admission, Raj is someone who likes to take charge. If we decide to go to dinner, he rings up and books a restaurant. If we need to clear up after cooking, he will galvanize everyone into action, handing out jobs and organizing the kitchen. It is as if he has a rule that says "Always take the lead." On one occasion we were discussing our ideas over breakfast with a group of other friends who had gathered for the weekend. Raj said that he didn't believe what we were saying was true for him and that he was sure he could choose any behavior he wanted. To prove the point, we decided to set him a challenge. We suggested that all he had to do was not take the lead in anything we did that day. He accepted the challenge. After the last slice of toast had been consumed, he stood up and said, without the slightest sense of irony, "Right, I'm not taking the lead, so Dave, you take the lead." Everyone erupted in laughter, apart from Raj, who was completely perplexed.

Not surprisingly, he was frustrated by the lack of decision makers in his business. He found that no matter what approaches he used to recruit new staff, he ended up with followers who wanted to be told what to do, rather than people who would take responsibility for making decisions. The culture of his business reflected his character and people soon found that the way things worked was that Raj took the lead. If people joined who had real leadership potential, they would soon clash with Raj and would either fit in with his way of working or, more often, leave.

If you have been walking in any upland area of Britain, you will have seen sheep tracks all over the fells. The sheep can wander anywhere they like, but they choose to stick to narrow paths, as if they are constrained by invisible fences. If our habitual behavior is like those sheep tracks, then our hidden rules are like those invisible fences. The more the sheep use those paths, the clearer they are and the less likely the animals are to stray from them.

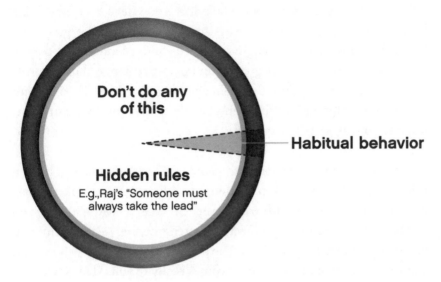

Figure 3 Habitual behavior and hidden rules

In any circumstance, a wide range of responses or ways of thinking and behaving are possible. Some will lead to a positive outcome, some won't. And yet, even when we know that the way we are behaving won't or can't achieve the result we want, we don't always choose the behavior that is helpful. We might see the other options that are available to us, but we never choose them. We don't even realize that we are making a choice.

YOUR STRENGTHS FLOW FROM HIDDEN RULES

Hidden rules do help us. They are the source of our strengths. There is a wealth of evidence that whatever we do repeatedly we become good at. Natural talent has its part to play, but the key factor, if we want to develop that talent, is putting in the hours of practice. Study after study has shown that what sets apart the star performers from the also-rans is the amount of time they devote to achieving excellence. Whether you want to be a concert violinist or take free kicks like David Beckham, you have to practice, practice, practice.

You have been practicing your whole life – you have been practicing thinking and behaving in the way that your hidden rules guide you to. If you look at your strengths, you will find a hidden rule behind each one. Whatever you are good at and pay attention to, a hidden rule has directed you to choose that behavior over all others. The behavior has become habitual and happens unconsciously and without effort because you are so practiced at it.

For example, if you are good with people you probably have a hidden rule that it is important to pay attention to how others think and feel and to build a rapport with whomever you meet. Because of this, you will have practiced all kinds of ways of strengthening relationships and have become very adept at them. The behavior needed to get along with people has become habitual and it comes easily to you. That is why it is one of your strengths. Similarly, if you are good at getting things done, you may have a hidden rule that it is important to see tasks through to the finish and have taken an interest in ways of improving your efficiency and effectiveness. With practice, the behaviors and ways of thinking that you need to get things done have become second nature.

Wherever you find a strength, you will also find a hidden rule. And if the game changes and you continue to play by the same rules, you will feel frustrated.

WHEN YOUR STRENGTHS BECOME LIMITATIONS

A strength is only a strength if it fits the situation, so your greatest strengths can, in some circumstances, become your greatest limitations. This is one of the main reasons for becoming stuck. This is what happened to Neil, who we described at the beginning of this chapter, and the water company from the previous chapter. Neil's strengths were his sharp mind and the attention he paid to winning the argument. They were also what led him to fail as a trainee barrister, as he failed to adapt his style. The water company's strength lay in its procedures to drive out risks, but this had stifled creativity and slowed the pace of change when the market changed.

We can think of hidden rules as keys that open certain doors. If a key fits the lock, we call it a good key. If it doesn't fit the lock, we call it a bad key. What the key looks like does not matter. The important question is whether it fits the lock. Similarly, if a hidden rule leads to actions that get you the results you want, then it's a powerful rule – why would you want to change it?

Your greatest strengths can in some circumstances become your greatest limitations

When your hidden rules are helpful to you, you get positive feedback in the form of affirmative emotions such as joy, happiness, excitement, peacefulness, and contentment. On the other hand, if your rules lead to actions that don't get you the results you want, then they are not helpful, and holding on to them will limit your ability to respond in a useful way. When your hidden rules limit you, you get feedback in the form of negative or afflictive emotions such as anger, fear, sadness, frustration, and bitterness.

Whether a particular behavior is a strength depends entirely on the context. Yet, so often, individuals and businesses fail to change because they are fixed in their thinking about what will contribute to success. Your real strengths are the ones you can let go of when circumstances require.

Malcolm worked as a senior manager in a government department. He had a talent for spotting what might go wrong, flowing from a hidden rule that said "Always look for the risks." Thinking in this way served him well in a political environment. He was seen as a good sounding board for any controversial plan. He was very bright and had a knack of spotting the flaws in a proposal before it became public or led to damaging publicity.

35

Malcolm had applied for a more senior position as chief executive of a government quango, one where he was expected to provide leadership for the whole organization. He was successful at the first stage of the selection process and was told privately by the recruitment consultants that he was way out in front going into the final stage. During the last interview, he was asked about his vision for the organization. Carefully and precisely, he set out everything that could go wrong with the organization and what he would do about it. Needless to say, he didn't get the job. His insight was perfect, but it wasn't what the recruitment panel were looking for in a new leader. The same rule that had served him well up to that point in his career had now become a major limitation. Everyone could see Malcolm's habits but Malcolm himself; his lack of self-awareness was what held him back. He didn't have the appetite to look deeply at his own ways of thinking and behaving and he changed his plans for his career.

We are not making judgments about whether any specific behavior is good or bad – that is not the point. The purpose of this example is to show that behavior that is helpful in one situation, is not going to get us anywhere in other circumstances. Your habits have developed for a good reason, usually because they have been rewarded in some way and they have brought you success. If you are good at generating ideas, you may well have worked in a job that has rewarded you for doing so. If you have a talent for listening, no doubt people have praised you for being a good listener. The problem comes when you bump up against the limits of these habits.

THREE KINDS OF HIDDEN RULES

Our hidden rules are often in conflict with the rules for success that we mentioned earlier. There are three ways they limit us that relate to the three Rs:

> **Unconscious intention** – our hidden rules limit what **results** we see as important to achieve and what we see as important to avoid

Limited awareness – our hidden rules limit what aspects of **reality** we should pay attention to and how to interpret what we perceive

Habitual action – our hidden rules limit how we **respond** or behave in order to achieve what is important

UNCONSCIOUS INTENTION

Because of our hidden rules we aren't free to decide what results we want. We have thoughts and ideas about what it is important to achieve and what it is important to avoid. We find it difficult to set goals that don't fit with these unconscious intentions. Unless you are aware of how your hidden rules determine the goals you set, they will be shaped by these unconscious thoughts about what is possible and impossible, what is desirable and undesirable.

THREE KINDS OF HIDDEN RULES

- Unconscious intention
- Limited awareness
- Habitual action

LIMITED AWARENESS

Because of our hidden rules, it is difficult to have a full and accurate understanding of our reality. We have unconscious thoughts about what we must pay attention to and how to interpret what we perceive. Due to these thoughts, we tend to notice those things that reinforce our own ideas and pay less attention to different ways of seeing things that challenge our views. Unless you are aware of how your hidden rules edit what you notice, you will miss important clues that can lead to a breakthrough. When you do see how your hidden rules limit your awareness, you can choose to step beyond their confines and develop curiosity about elements that do not fit with your own story of the way things are. You can then choose to act in ways that fit the broader reality rather than merely your own limited version.

HABITUAL ACTION

Because of our hidden rules we aren't free to choose the best response to a given situation. We have unconscious thoughts about what actions or behaviors we see as acceptable or useful regardless of the circumstances. When you do become aware of the ways in which your hidden rules limit your actions, you are more likely to have the ability to choose your response when a situation arises in which your habitual behavior doesn't give you the best outcome.

An example can help demonstrate how hidden rules work and how identifying them can help. Tom was a trainer working in a medium-sized IT training company. He really knew his stuff, but he simply wasn't getting the results he wanted with his trainees. During a discussion about what he liked about his work and what he found difficult, he repeatedly said things such as "You can't let anyone feel uncomfortable" and "You mustn't put people on the spot." When he was challenged about these statements, he responded with "Doesn't everyone think that?"

He was surprised when some of the other trainers he was with said that they felt it was important to put people on the spot and that they knew they were getting somewhere when people felt stretched by what they were learning. When asked what he thought the consequences would be of letting people feel uncomfortable, he found it difficult to answer. "It's just not the right thing to do!" he exclaimed – a sure sign of a hidden rule. When pressed, he said that he felt people didn't like it when they were in the spotlight and that everything would go wrong. "What if they get upset?" he asked. Whenever any of his trainees experienced difficulty caused by a lack of understanding, Tom would quickly move on or cover the discomfort by providing the answers, so reducing the opportunity for learning.

What Tom started to spot through this questioning process were his hidden rules and the behaviors that flow from them. These were the hidden rules he identified:

⟫ **Unconscious intention** – *people mustn't feel uncomfortable.* Tom dislikes the idea of anyone feeling uncomfortable. This could well be because of his own discomfort at being in the spotlight as a trainer. He is quite introverted and has to work hard to overcome his shyness at being in front of the group. He projects his own lack of ease onto his trainees.

⟶ **Limited awareness** – *people always feel uncomfortable when they don't know the answers.* We discovered that Tom is extremely uncomfortable when he doesn't know the answer to a question. He notices his own discomfort and assumes that other people must feel the same way. He fails to notice that many people learn more when they have to think for themselves.

⟶ **Habitual action** – *cover any discomfort by providing answers or using humor.* When anyone looks like they might not know the answer to a question or struggles with an exercise, he quickly intervenes and so reduces the opportunity for learning. He uses humor to cover up difficulties or disagreements, which means that the groups he is working with don't have the chance to explore challenging issues.

Tom had never investigated his thoughts in this way before. He had simply believed that what he thought was "the truth," obvious and true for all people at all times. His approach made him a likeable person, very easy to get along with. This way of thinking also really took the edge off his ability as a trainer. What was revealing was seeing how uncomfortable he himself was when he was in the spotlight.

Following some coaching sessions, Tom started to look objectively at these rules and see that they were merely thoughts and not universal truths. The examples provided by other experienced trainers gave him a good starting point for challenging his own thinking. He could see that there were some circumstances in which his ideas were helpful and some in which they weren't, particularly in the training room. He started to explore how he could let his trainees learn more effectively when they were uncertain and pushing at the boundaries of their own knowledge. He developed a positive message about stretching people that he could affirm to himself before he went into the training room. He examined what behavior flowed from his hidden rules and practiced new ways of behaving, such as reflecting difficult questions back to the trainee rather than immediately answering them. He learned from other trainers who were good role models of the kind of behavior he wanted to adopt. The rules didn't go away, but they had less of a hold on his behavior and he made a breakthrough in his ability as a trainer as a result.

HIDDEN RULES AND DO-HOW

Helen, a manager responsible for IT at a large clothing retailer, ran separate IT teams at two different sites. One team was working well and delivering results, but the other team had repeatedly failed to deliver on deadlines and there had been a couple of embarrassing problems where key IT services had been temporarily unavailable due to avoidable errors. We met separately with Helen, Helen's boss, and her team to assess the situation and help her find a way forward.

Helen's boss had told us that Helen was a good manager so long as it didn't mean having to challenge underperformance in her team. "She likes to get along with everyone and when she does she gets the best out of people," he said. "But one of her team, Frank, applied for the same job as her and didn't get it. He resents Helen being promoted over him and he causes all sorts of problems for her. Until she sorts that out, she won't get the team performing. I could step in, but I want her to learn how to handle this for herself."

This view was confirmed by other members of the team. We heard comments like "Helen spends all her time dancing around Frank trying to keep him on board," "Some people don't always work for the good of the team," and "Helen is lovely but some team members take advantage of her."

The dialogue below is based on the conversation Dave had with Helen. Helen has already agreed that her goal is to tackle Frank's performance, to get him working well with the rest of the team and sticking to agreed priorities. During the conversation, Dave is using the three Rs to help Helen identify a breakthrough. See if you can spot Helen's hidden rules and how they limit her.

Dave: So how do you see the situation now? What's getting in the way? (*reality*)
Helen: Frank takes up more of my time than anyone. He's good at what he does, but he seems to have his own ideas about what is important. I sometimes feel like if I tell him a job is a priority he finds a way to avoid doing what I want him to do. It's important to me to get everyone working well together,

but he doesn't always support other team members in the way I would like. I seem to spend most of my time either trying to get him on board with the rest of the team or dealing with the fallout. I've had so many conversations with him about his behavior. (*reality, needs a breakthrough*)

Dave: So what do you need to do now? (*response*)

Helen: I need to have another word with Frank. He has to realize that he's got to buck up his ideas. I've offered him whatever support he needs, but he's got to get on board with the rest of the team. (*habitual response*)

Dave: Do you think that will work? From what you have said you've tried talking to him. (*challenging the habitual response*)

Helen: I'm not sure what else I can do. I can see how difficult it is for him given that he wanted my job and I'm willing to offer him whatever support he needs to help him work well with the rest of the team. I need his cooperation for some of the key projects he's got on. If I lose his support we would have a real problem. I don't want to push too hard. (*feels stuck, habitual response*)

Dave: Let's imagine we get back together in six months' time. How confident are you that having a word with Frank will make any difference to his behavior? (*challenging the habitual response*)

Helen: If you put it that way, less than 10 percent, I suppose. I've tried everything with him but he doesn't want to play ball. I need his expertise, though. He is the only one who really understands some of our systems. I feel between a rock and a hard place. (*reality, feels stuck, experiences negative emotions*)

Dave: Is there anything else you could do? (*Inviting alternative response*)

Helen: I'm not sure if I want to put him in a disciplinary process. It just doesn't seem right. (*negative emotions*)

Dave: Why not? From what you've said he's simply not performed the way you would expect someone in his position to. (*challenging her awareness of her reality*)

Helen: It would feel disloyal. He's been a member of this team for longer than I have. There must be some way of helping him with this. I've always got on with the people I've worked with. I'd feel uncomfortable. (*negative emotions, limited by her strengths*)

Dave: Do you feel comfortable with the situation now? (*challenging her awareness of her reality*)

Helen: I guess not. (*negative emotions*)

Dave: So what is the real problem? (*challenging her awareness of her reality*)

Helen: I know he's a pain, but I really do want to help him. (*negative emotions, habitual response*)

Dave: You've tried helping him, but will that work if it isn't what he wants? (*challenging habitual response*)

Helen: I could discipline him, but what do I do if he goes off sick or refuses to cooperate? (*considers alternative response*)

Dave: It sounds like he's already refusing to cooperate. As for going off sick, what would you normally do if he did? Suppose one of your team needed an operation and was away for a couple of months, what would you do then? (*encouraging alternative response*)

Helen: We'd get in a contractor. I hadn't really thought about that. (*alternative response*)

Dave: Could you do that if Frank went off sick? (*encouraging alternative response*)

Helen: Yes, of course. (*starts to buy in to alternative response*)

Dave: Is there anything else?

Helen: I need to understand our disciplinary procedures and make sure I'm on solid ground. I also need to make sure I've got the backing of my boss. (*getting more excited about the alternative response*)

Dave: Given that he suggested this conversation, do you think he would back you? (*reality*)

Helen: Yes. I'm pretty certain that this is what he wants anyway. (*reality*)

Dave: How confident do you feel about giving this approach a try? (*encouraging alternative response*)

Helen: Actually, now we've talked it over it seems like it's the obvious thing to do. I feel like a weight has been lifted from my shoulders. I've been ground down by this situation. but I can see a way forward.

We can spot Helen's hidden rules at play during the conversation and how these prevent her from doing what she knows she needs to do:

⟩ **Unconscious intention**. Helen's habitual thought is *I must keep the team together*. That's why she finds the idea of disciplining Frank so difficult. She wants everyone to get along and work together well. This has been an asset to her and most of her team love working for her, but this approach won't be productive with a disaffected team member. Her unconscious goal overrides her explicit goal of having a well-functioning team.

▥➔ **Limited awareness**. Helen's habitual thought is *What support do people need?* She is tuned in to notice where people are struggling and where they need support. This has really helped her in the past. People feel valued by her and this means that she gets the best out of them. However, it now means that she is concentrating more and more time on Frank, although with few returns. It also means that she has less time for the rest of the team or for the other things she has to do to be a good all-round manager. She is so focused on helping Frank that she has lost sight of the bigger picture.

▥➔ **Habitual action**. Helen's habitual action is *Support people to get the best out of them.* She can be relied on to take people under her wing and nurture them, or to muck in if there is an urgent need for help. While this creates a great atmosphere in the teams she works in and has been one of her greatest strengths, she can't make progress in this situation using that approach. Frank is undermining her and dragging the team down. Her boss can see this and so can the team. Helen finds it difficult to consider another approach and can't imagine that she could get by without Frank. Unless she can adapt her behavior, she will continue to find the situation impossible.

With a little more coaching, Helen tried the approach she had agreed with Dave and, to no one's surprise, Frank decided to leave a few months later for another job. Helen learned a great deal from the experience. She found that her team and other colleagues respected her all the more for taking a firm line with Frank. She also found that the team blossomed and that she enjoyed her work more than she had done in years. Her boss was delighted that she had stepped up to the mark and taken on a tough situation.

In the grand scheme of things, finding the courage to discipline an underperforming team member might seem like a small breakthrough. After all, isn't that what anyone would learn how to do on a basic management training program? For Helen, though, it was a big breakthrough. In taking this step she transformed how she saw herself. She remains a caring and supportive manager, but she is no longer scared of dealing with unacceptable behavior. What is as important is the effect that her breakthrough had on the rest of the organization. One of the reasons we had been asked to help is that her boss had identified a failure to deal with underperforming team members as one of the reasons his division was struggling. The way Helen changed provided a role model for other managers in her division. So it wasn't only a breakthrough for her, it was a breakthrough for the business, demonstrating the do-how the organization needed and contributing to a wider shift in culture.

CHANGE IS ALWAYS POSSIBLE

When you see someone make the kind of breakthrough that Helen did, you can't fail to notice the enormous impact it has not merely on them but also on the people around them. You might wonder if this kind of breakthrough is possible for you or in your organization. In our experience, change is always possible, provided that you really want the change and you have the courage to face and own the role of your thinking and behavior in creating and sustaining your problems and difficulties. What is more, it is possible to learn some simple steps that will inevitably lead you to making this kind of breakthrough.

Change is always possible

In the following pages we will show you four simple, tried-and-tested steps that lead from know-how to do-how. We will also demonstrate how these same steps can be applied not only to personal breakthroughs but to create lasting changes in teams and throughout large organizations.

TRY THIS: WHO CHOOSES YOUR BEHAVIOR?

You may think that what we are saying in this chapter doesn't apply to you. This exercise will help you find out.

Make a list of your strengths or qualities. For example, you might see yourself as decisive or helpful or as having a good sense of humor. Be as specific as you can.

Choose one of the strengths you have listed and try going through the day without exercising this quality. If you like to crack jokes, try going without making a joke for a day. If you are the sort of person who likes to impress people, try a day where you don't impress people. Let them know what you are doing so that you can get their feedback later.

This will feel uncomfortable and the chances are that you will find it much more difficult than you expect. You may find your mind coming up with all sorts of reasons why this is a stupid exercise or is not worth doing. Whatever happens, it is important that you make a note of what you experience. Take a little time at the end of the day to reflect on what happened. What were your thoughts and feelings? How did people respond? What did other people think of how you did?

Chapter 3

THE DO-HOW MAP
How to develop do-how

In India, elephants were once commonly used for heavy lifting and it was important that they were easy to control. An elephant rampaging through the streets could do enormous amounts of damage and would be a serious threat to life. It would take a very heavy chain to tie an elephant up, and so the trainers, called *mahouts*, came up with a cunning way to keep the animals from straying.

Starting when the elephant was young, they would put a chain around its leg and tie the other end to a strong stake in the ground. The young animal would try to wander off, but was not yet strong enough to break the chain or pull the stake from the ground. Over a few weeks, the youngster would come to learn that its attempts to wander were futile, resulting only in a sharp and sometimes painful tug on the leg. After a while, it would make no further attempts to wander. By the time the elephant was fully grown, it had learned to stay within a few feet of the stake, and all the *mahout* had to do was drive a stake into the ground and attach a light chain to the elephant's ankle.

Although this practice might seem a little harsh on the elephant, it was clearly effective. We, too, have received training about limitations, whether intended or not. We have felt pain or experienced discomfort and learned that there are limits that we had better not step over, or we will receive a nasty jolt. Therefore we do not have the freedom to set our own goals, to notice what is there to be noticed, or to choose our own actions. Because of this, we do not realize our potential. However, these limits, learned in our formative years, need be no more restrictive today than the *mahout*'s chains on the full-grown elephant.

What really limits you is your ignorance of the limitations placed on your thinking and behavior by your hidden rules

What really limits us and leads to us getting stuck is ignorance of the limitations placed on our thinking and behavior by our hidden rules. When we finally see the constraints that our rules have set around and about us, we can also see that the those limitations are only there in our mind. They are restrictions that we put on ourselves, they are not imposed from outside.

We are not saying that with self-awareness you'll be able to do the impossible. What you certainly will be able to do, in fact won't be able to stop yourself doing, is to redefine what you see as possible. When you see this for yourself, you will have the freedom to choose your behavior and any breakthrough you want to make will become possible.

EASY TO SAY, HARD TO DO

To make a breakthrough you need to respond in a way that is consistent with the result you want to achieve given the reality. That is where the three Rs can help.

If you look back at the examples we have given so far – Helen, Tom, Malcolm, Teri, Alan, and Geoff's team – you can see that each of them faced a choice. They could continue to behave out of habit, or they could deal with their discomfort and change their behavior in a way that was more likely to get the result they wanted. For any outcome we want, there will be dozens of different things we could do, but the one that most readily comes to hand is our habitual response. That is fine if it gets us the result we want. If you are getting the outcome you want, why would you want to change that?

But what happens when, like Helen or the others, your hidden rules deter you from choosing a behavior that can really help? What Helen faced when she wrestled with her discomfort at confronting Frank is what we call a do-how moment. When you try to make a breakthrough, you will reach a fork in the road where your choices make a difference. You have a decision between your habitual behavior and the behavior that will get you the results you want. What you choose to do in that do-how moment will determine whether you make a breakthrough or remain stuck.

Nevertheless, this understates the challenge. Your habitual patterns of behavior are like a six-lane highway, while any new way of behaving that you want to adopt can seem more like a narrow country lane. You might have the know-how and set out with good intentions to take a different

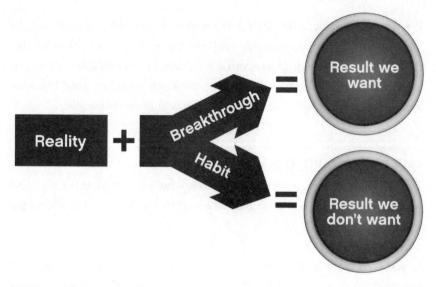

Figure 4 The do-how moment

approach, the way you know will lead to a breakthrough for you, but before you know where you are you've gone down the well-trodden path and done the very things that you know aren't really in your interests.

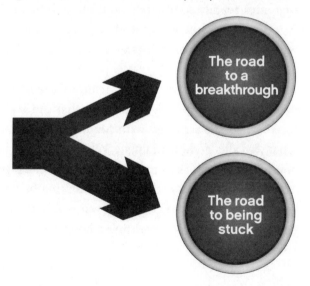

Figure 5 The difficulty in making a breakthrough

The upward fork in Figure 5 represents the behavior or actions that will get you the results you want. In the example of Helen, her positive intention is to deal with Frank in a way that leads to him changing his behavior or leaving for another job. The lower fork is the behavior that is leading to you being stuck. In Helen's case, this means remaining stuck in trying to support Frank and avoiding the really difficult conversation. She had already identified that she needed to take a stronger approach with Frank, but she also found it much easier to take the downward fork rather than do what she intended. She somehow kept on being hijacked by her own desire to help and support Frank and avoid a tough conversation.

> The real breakthrough is to choose your behavior

The three Rs model we shared in the previous chapter is useful, but is not enough on its own. While it is intellectually rigorous, it doesn't necessarily lead to a breakthrough, merely an idea of what a breakthrough looks like. The real breakthrough happens when you let go of your habits and act in a way that is consistent with the results you want. In other words, the real breakthrough is to choose your behavior. That is what leads to do-how.

EMOTIONS POLICE OUR RULES

There is a further difficulty to deal with when making this choice. At the very moments when we need to choose a different behavior, we experience strong negative emotions, which drive us toward our habitual behavior. If you look back at Helen, Tom, Teri, or Alan, you can see their discomfort at letting go of their habitual response. Our emotions are like a wake-up call that tells us a line is about to be crossed and that one of our rules is about to be broken.

Our emotions point to hidden thoughts. An emotion is a message to do something, a cause of motion or action. The emotions associated with each of our hidden rules remind us to act in a way that is in line with that rule. This is just like the elephant's chains. We can easily break our own rules in the same way that the adult elephant can break the chains but, in both cases, fear prevents us from doing so.

51

Our rules are the guide rails along which our lives run. If we are doing something that is within our rules, we feel happy. As soon as something happens that takes us outside our rules or challenges some deep-seated and unexamined thought, we feel uncomfortable. That is what our emotions are there for. They remind us when we are straying outside the comfort zone provided by our rules. They are internal feedback, telling us "Watch out, something might happen here that you won't like." The more deeply seated and hidden our rules are, the more likely we are to experience a strong, and perhaps to others irrational, discomfort when that aspect of our thinking or behavior is challenged.

For example, you might have noticed that one of Alan's hidden rules was to polish his ideas until he came up with the perfect plan. What do you think would happen if he were put on the spot and forced to make a difficult choice? Suppose one of his directors came to him with an ultimatum: "Make a choice right now about the direction of the organization, or I go." You can bet your shirt that Alan would experience a negative emotion. He would feel pressurized, would want more time, and would no doubt see the director as being "difficult."

This relationship between our emotions and our hidden rules is crucial and gives us a way to spot our do-how moments. Most of the time we assume that our emotions are simply a reaction to circumstances and that anyone would feel the same way. However, we need to appreciate that they point to moments when our rules are being challenged – at least some of those moments will be do-how moments, when our choices can make a real difference.

THE DO-HOW MAP

We need a way of helping us choose the upward fork in those moments. Luckily, there are four steps anyone can take to make it easier to choose the breakthrough rather than being limited by hidden rules. These make up what we call the *do-how map*, which can help you move from know-how to do-how. The four steps are:

Recognize your do-how moments

Spell out the breakthrough you want

Uncover your hidden rules

Take responsibility for your choices

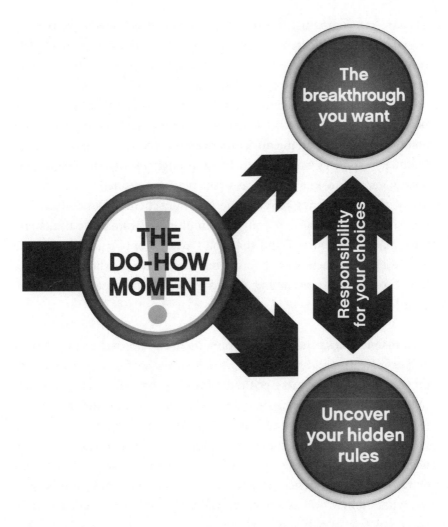

Figure 6   The do-how map

RECOGNIZE YOUR DO-HOW MOMENTS

The most important thing you can do to open up this choice is to recognize that the discomfort you feel points to the fact that you have a choice. There are moments when your choices can move you from know-how to do-how. What you choose to do in that moment either perpetuates the existing situation or takes you beyond the limited ways in which you think and behave to create change and deliver results.

The key to recognizing the do-how moment is to acknowledge that any negative or uncomfortable emotion points to the possibility of a breakthrough. Discomfort in the form of anxiety, fear, anger, frustration, sadness, or any other negative emotion can be seen as a signpost telling you that you have reached the limit of your habits and that you have the power to choose another way. By understanding and owning your own emotional reactions to the difficulties you meet, you can overcome your habitual responses and make a breakthrough in any challenge. This means getting to know the ways you react emotionally to situations and, rather than trying to resist them or fight them off, understanding that they are a signal that you are bumping up against the limits you have placed on yourself and that you have the opportunity to choose a different approach. By becoming more sensitive to when those emotional reactions are occurring, you can develop the capacity to choose your behavior.

This insight bucks the trend in some modern approaches to personal and organizational development, which encourage us to focus entirely on the positive. Of course positive psychology can be highly motivating, but in our experience it is often when individuals and teams confront their deepest fears and insecurities that the true breakthroughs are made. The reality is that most people experience a whole range of negative emotions in the course of a typical day or week and you can employ those experiences to positive ends. We will show you how to use what bothers you as a wake-up call that can create choice and help you break free of habitual and cultural limits.

SPELL OUT THE BREAKTHROUGH YOU WANT

The second action you can take is to spell out the breakthrough you want in terms of precise outcomes and, most importantly, your own specific behavior. Whatever breakthrough you want to make, it's likely that a change of behavior is needed that is likely to be in competition with the way you behave at the moment. This usually means finding out what the do-how you need looks like in practice. The more vividly you can bring this to life, the more chance there is that you will make the right choices when they arrive.

We will show you how you can picture the positive, precise possibility for the breakthrough you want. By being clear about the change in behavior you intend to make and what this behavior looks like in practice, you can make it easier to step beyond the habitual ways of thinking and behaving. This also means practicing a new way of behaving, which effectively makes the upper fork larger and more accessible. The more you practice, the easier it will be for you to choose that behavior when you want to or need to.

For Tom, whom we mentioned earlier, this meant understanding that his goal was to let his trainees learn and to have a clear picture of how he could behave when one of his trainees felt uncomfortable. He could achieve this by looking at role models who successfully use this approach and finding out how they think and behave.

UNCOVER YOUR HIDDEN RULES

It is difficult to let go of something that you don't know you are holding on to. It is not enough to know that you have hidden rules, you need to know what they are. Unless the unconscious choices you are making and the thoughts behind them are uncovered and brought to conscious awareness, they will always hijack any efforts to choose a different approach. When you get them clearly in view, you can see what you need to let go of.

We will set out practical ways in which you can identify your own habitual ways of thinking and behaving or how the culture of your organization limits behavior. The deeper you can go and the more you can bring your hidden rules into consciousness and understand the deep-seated needs that they satisfy, the more powerful your ability to change will be. This helps to define precisely what the downward pointing fork looks, sounds, and feels like. The more familiar you are with your hidden rules, and with how they guide your unconscious intentions, limit your awareness, and lead to habitual behavior, the easier it is to relinquish them when they come calling.

TAKE RESPONSIBILITY FOR YOUR CHOICES

The final step is to take total responsibility for choosing to act in a way that is consistent with the breakthrough you want rather than acting out of your emotional need. Your habits don't give up without a fight. It takes emotional maturity and courage to face up to deep-seated and long-held thoughts about what is right and useful behavior. One of the most common ways in which people sabotage their own success is by blaming other people or events for the problems and difficulties they face. This attitude makes them powerless and leaves them thinking that there is nothing they can do. By understanding how you make yourself into a victim of your situation, you can leverage your own capacity for change.

We will show you how to transform feelings of powerlessness into the ability to take responsibility and turn any adversity into a source of advantage.

Recognizing your do-how moments is about acknowledging that you have a choice in how you respond to situations and that these choices occur at moments when you feel uncomfortable. You can respond in a way that lines up with the change you want to make, but only if you are clear what this looks like. This is the upward fork. You also need to let go of your habitual behavior, and you can only do this if you understand your hidden rules and how they limit the choices you make. The final step is to appreciate that this choice only opens up if you take total responsibility for your choices. If you see yourself as a passive victim of circumstances, it is likely that you will feel powerless to act and your choices will not be apparent to you.

The do-how map is a practical way to summarize all of the key steps that anyone can take to ensure the best possible success in any change. In the following chapters we set out in more detail how you can use the do-how map to break free of the habits and cultural norms that limit you and make the changes you want.

THE DO-HOW MAP
* Recognize your do-how moments
* Spell out the breakthrough you want
* Uncover your hidden rules
* Take responsibility for your choices

TRY THIS: TEST YOUR DO-HOW MAP

Think of a specific situation where you want to choose a different response. You might think about what you wrote in the first exercise in this book. Choose something that matters to you and that is also challenging for you.

Map out your choice in that moment, similar to the do-how map in Figure 6.

What is the breakthrough behavior? What result will that behavior give you that you aren't getting at the moment?

What is your habitual response in that situation? What do you normally do? What are the consequences of that choice?

Have a go at making this choice in practice. Choose a specific date and time when you know you will be faced with this choice, perhaps a meeting with someone you find difficult.

The do-how map isn't only something written on a piece of paper. It's your experience of what happens when you try to make a change. Don't merely think about this, but make a commitment to test what happens sometime soon by consciously choosing the upper fork.

What happened?

What emotions did you experience? What thoughts did you have?

If you were to adopt this behavior consistently, what would the benefits be for you? What difference would it make to your work and life?

On a scale of 1 to 10, how difficult is it for you to choose the upward fork consistently?

What areas of the do-how map do you most need to focus on to make a breakthrough?

Chapter 4

FROM BOTHER TO
BREAKTHROUGH
How to recognize your
do-how moments

THE
DO-HOW
MOMENT
!

An old friend of ours called Jeff lived in a rambling farmhouse on a small country lane that led off from a long, straight road. Each time we visited Jeff we would inevitably whiz past the turning for his house before realizing where we were and would have to turn around in the car park of the Red Lion pub, half a mile further up the road. There was a small sign on the lane, but it had long been overgrown and become part of the hedge, visible only if you parked next to it and parted the leaves with your hands. If the pub had been a half a mile before the turning that would have been a great help, as it would have provided us with something to look out for. Even though we would remind ourselves to look out for the turning, there simply weren't any discernible landmarks, only miles of hedges with the odd oak tree. At least that was the way it seemed to us, until Jeff pointed out that there was one tree with a broken branch that looked like a hitch-hiker's thumb stuck out for passing traffic about a hundred yards before the lane. Once we knew to look out for that as our signpost, we never missed the turning again.

There are moments when your choices can lead you to a breakthrough –
do-how moments

There are moments when your choices can lead you to a breakthrough. But you need a signpost, something that lets you know that you're approaching one of those moments and that you have a choice. Do you stay on the main road that leads to the same old problems, or do you take the narrow turning that leads to a breakthrough? Fortunately, you have just such a signpost once it is pointed out to you. That signpost is your own discomfort at the difficulties you face.

Remember that whenever an uncomfortable emotion arises, this indicates that one of your hidden rules is being challenged or broken. We'd rather not experience these emotions. We tend to see negative emotions as undesirable and we usually try to avoid them, or at least retreat from them at the first opportunity. The emotion is effectively saying, "You need to do something now to enforce your rules." However, when we are stuck the emotion tends to push us toward the very ways of behaving that led us to being stuck in the first place. That's when we need a breakthrough. The very fact that you are bothered by a situation points to the opportunity for a breakthrough. This is what we mean by the do-how moment.

When a hidden rule kicks in, you know that you aren't really choosing your behavior but are acting habitually in the way the rule leads you to behave. At this point there are only two possibilities. Either your hidden rules and the behavior that flows from them get you the results you want, in which case you wouldn't want to do anything differently; or you aren't getting the results you want and you need to change. In these circumstances your hidden rules are preventing you from making the choices that represent a breakthrough. If you can spot the times when you are bothered by a situation *and* you aren't getting the results you want, that tells you that you have a choice that can lead to the change you want.

So when you feel a negative emotion, or observe one in another person, think of it as a signpost to tell you a choice is coming up. You can act out of the emotion you are experiencing and choose the downward fork. Or you can act in line with the breakthrough you want to make and choose the upward fork. It's your choice. The alternative is for your response to choose you, as you react out of your emotion, out of habit. That's how we get stuck: we intend to make a choice, but we act in line with our hidden rules. Let's see how this works.

ACTING OUT OF INTENTION OR OUT OF EMOTION

Some years ago we worked with a large, publicly listed investment company that was going through a crisis and needed a rapid change in direction. The company had a portfolio of property investments in the United States, Australia, and New Zealand, but had also invested heavily in racehorses and stud properties and had become well known as a favorite investment for those interested in thoroughbred horses. Unfortunately, while these bloodstock investments were considered sexy and newsworthy, they had consistently failed to provide an adequate return and the company seemed destined to collapse if its corporate strategy continued. Despite repeated resolutions by the board to take the company in a new direction, the strategy had not changed significantly over the previous three years. Financial data suggested that the investments would continue to take money out of the company in the year ahead and push the business into insolvency. The media were starting to speculate about the state of the company and at least one television company had investigative journalists asking unwelcome questions.

A bright and dynamic chief executive had been recruited to rescue the company and his assessment of the situation was swift and simple. It must dispose of its loss-making bloodstock assets in a carefully controlled manner and reposition itself by increasing its property assets. In the eyes of the new chief executive and several of his fellow directors, this choice was a "no-brainer." It was obvious what to do, just as it had been obvious for the previous three years.

The do-how moment came when the board gathered to consider the proposal. The chairman was a highly respected and nationally known senior businessman. Several other board members also had national profiles, with seats on the boards of numerous publicly listed companies between them. Given the caliber of the directors, the new chief executive expected that his proposal would go through without requiring any serious debate. To his surprise, the meeting was long, fractious, and inconclusive. The board seemed unable to take this simple, obvious decision. Bewildered, the chief executive asked them to meet again later in the week.

That second meeting, held at a swanky, ocean-side hotel on the Pacific coast of California, went on well into the night. The directors had few detailed concerns about the proposed change in investment strategy. The figures spoke for themselves: carry on with the existing bloodstock strategy and go broke, or change direction and live to fight another day. The real issue, it emerged, was their fears, particularly fears about reputation. As the evening wore on, it became clear that the essential worry for the chairman and board members was that their personal reputations were on the line. They had taken the company in this direction and now it was in trouble.

The do-how map for the board looked like this:

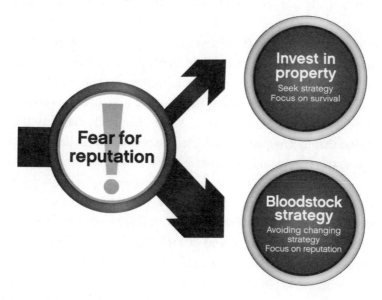

Figure 7   Investment company do-how map

The exclamation mark in the middle indicates the emotional reaction of various board members when faced with a decision that could tarnish their reputations. They experienced fear that they would appear to have involved the company in an unsuccessful investment strategy. This focus on reputation was part of what had made the company successful in the past. However, clinging on to that was now leading the board to make poor choices. They were at a do-how moment. What they chose to do in that moment would either reinforce their discomfort or help them achieve what they really wanted, a thriving company.

Members of the board weren't necessarily aware that they were experiencing these feelings at the time. In fact, they only became aware of how they felt when the chief executive raised the issue of reputation. Their fear of losing their reputation drove them down the path of avoiding the difficult decision to sell off their more glamorous assets. They were in danger of acting out of emotion rather than in line with their explicit intention. This might have helped them achieve an unconscious goal of temporarily looking good in the eyes of others, but it wasn't delivering what they really wanted, which was a sound investment company.

What is important is that the emotional reaction was a signpost that their hidden rules were limiting them and that there was a difficult choice to make if they wanted to achieve a breakthrough. By pointing this out and helping them to articulate their fears, the chief executive was able to help them see the consequences of their choices. Ironically, the very focus on reputation that had helped the company grow was now in danger of taking it down a path that would lead to irrecoverable damage to that reputation.

Once these fears were aired, the board was able to reflect on the potential impact on reputation of the choices represented on the do-how map in Figure 7. At that point, it was straightforward to see that changing the investment strategy would minimize reputational damage, albeit with some humble pie to be eaten in the process. The board took the decision to dispose of its racehorses and other loss-making properties and as a result the company went on to thrive in the growing property market at that time.

EMOTIONS ARE EVERYWHERE

You might think that all this talk of emotions only applies to more sensitive or demonstrative people. However, we want to emphasize the extent to which everyone experiences both positive and negative emotions each and every day. Some people don't see themselves as emotional and indeed, there are those who rarely display their emotions. Nevertheless, whether they are acknowledged or unrecognized, expressed or repressed, the reality is that emotions are everywhere.

There is a widely believed myth that the Inuit language has hundreds of words for different types of snow. This myth continues largely because it seems to make sense to us that snow would be important to the people of the frozen north of Canada and Alaska. Now consider that many academics list as many as 4,000 words and phrases in the English language to express the subtleties of emotion, and you start to get a glimpse of just how important a role emotion plays in our lives.

There are many negative or afflictive emotions. Some of the most common are anger, frustration, fear, grief, sadness, dejection, envy, jealousy, boredom, pessimism, irritation, and hatred. These are in contrast to the pleasant or positive emotions, such as joy, happiness, pleasure, appreciation, contentment, excitement, inspiration, peacefulness, gladness, comfort, delight, optimism, hope, and many others. We are all quite familiar with these emotions, even if we aren't conscious of them. If you are sensitive to them in yourself and in those around you, you will realize that you rarely get through a day without experiencing at least one emotion.

We would argue that as soon as a few people are together, there are bound to be some negative emotions flying around, even among those who get on well. When a lot is at stake – an important meeting, or a difficult conversation – negative emotions will be running high, whether we notice and acknowledge them or not. Just reflect on the past week, even when you've been alone in your office. An email arrives, perhaps blaming you for something or other, and before you know it the red mist has descended and off goes a flaming reply.

Can you spot times when you have experienced a negative emotion? We are not necessarily talking here about extremities of emotion. Anger, for example, ranges from mild irritation and frustration through to full-blown rage and fury. You may experience or witness rage very rarely, but when was the last time you passed a whole day without any signs of irritation? If you have, you are living a rather idyllic lifestyle, in our view.

We also see negative emotions in other people, if we are looking for them. When we observe or notice negative emotions in others, this tells us that their hidden rules, their deep-seated and underlying motivations, are being challenged.

Positive emotions, in contrast, tell us that we are on track. They point to the upper fork of the do-how map, just as negative emotions point to the downward fork. And this upward fork leads to a breakthrough, something that you are attracted to and excited by, that will make you feel happy. If you don't feel excited and energized by the breakthrough, you probably haven't got it right. Knowing what energizes you can help you to identify what the upward fork looks like.

THERE'S A DO-HOW MOMENT COMING UP

What is remarkable about using emotions as a signpost is that you can spot your do-how moments in advance. Suppose you have a regular meeting with someone you find frustrating or annoying. Every time you meet that person you end up tearing your hair out, because you can't make progress or they don't listen or whatever it is that gets to you. You know that the emotion will arise and if you want to change things, then that is a do-how moment. You can plan in advance a different approach that might get better results.

The fact that we can predict when our do-how moments will arise shouldn't be surprising, since the emotional reactions that point to the do-how moments are associated with our habitual behavior, which we tend to repeat again and again, creating similar situations for ourselves. The person who gets angry when they can't get their own way knows in advance that when faced with a situation when they are thwarted, they will experience anger. They don't have to spot the anger in the heat of the moment, they know that it's coming and can rehearse what to do before it arises. All they have to do is notice that the emotion is there.

TRY THIS: RECOGNIZE A DO-HOW MOMENT

Reflect on a difficult or challenging situation where you experienced a negative emotion. (It can be helpful to think of an emotion you experience regularly or a situation you might experience again in the future.) Make a few notes detailing the following:

What happened?

What was your emotion?

When did you notice your emotional reaction? Before, during, or after?

What could you do differently if you faced the same situation again today?

SPOTTING EMOTIONS IN PRACTICE

Recognizing negative and positive emotions in advance can be really helpful. Eva was a senior manager in a pharmaceutical company who attended a development program that we delivered. In the dialogue below, Dave is leading Eva through the do-how map to help her make a significant breakthrough with a problem that has held her back.

Dave: Tell me what breakthrough you want to make, Eva.

Eva: I've got to give a speech at a major conference in a few weeks and I'm dreading it. I'll be speaking to an audience of over 1,000 people. Public speaking has always filled me with dread. I've been on various training programs about how to give great presentations, but I always feel the same afterward.

Dave: When you say it fills you with dread, what specifically happens when you think about giving the presentation?

Eva: I've experienced this before. I get a knot in my stomach and my mouth goes dry. I feel like I'm going to dry up and look stupid in front of my peers in the industry. I don't want people to judge me or think that I don't know my stuff.

I try to carry on, but the presentation becomes very stilted and I keep losing my train of thought.

Dave: So, what would you say you want?

Eva: Not looking stupid would be a good start. I've done quite a lot of presentations and so on with my work, but rarely to an audience of this size and with so many knowledgeable people.

Dave: Is that really what you want? Could you state that positively?

Eva: I suppose I really want to give a great presentation and for everyone to think it was a great presentation.

Dave: And what is it like when you picture yourself giving a great presentation? What happens?

Eva: I feel that I know my subject. I'm relaxed and know I can handle any questions that come up.

Dave: I see. We could ask more questions about that, but I just want to know, when you say that you think people will judge you, who will judge you and how will they judge you?

Eva: I don't know, everyone, I suppose. I mean, what if I say something stupid or get my facts wrong? There will be lots of people who know more than I do in that audience. They might think I don't know my stuff.

Dave: Eva, let me ask you, why were you asked to give this presentation?

Eva: Our organization has done some ground-breaking work over the last couple of years and people in the industry want to know about it.

Dave: Okay. So why were you specifically asked?

Eva: I suppose because I know more than anyone else about what we've been doing and the results we've been getting. I see where you are going with this.

Dave: So we know that the emotion you experience is dread and with that dread comes the knot in your stomach and the dry mouth. Behind that emotion is a thought, the thought that people will judge you. This leads to you losing your train of thought. Now, what's the rule that forces you to choose this fork rather than the upper fork?

Eva: I'm not sure. I don't really know what you mean by a rule. It just happens.

Dave: It sounds like you want to know everything, Eva. Or at least you want to know more than everyone else. Does it sound familiar if you say to yourself, "I have to know more than everyone else?"

Eva: Oh my goodness, that's what my brother always says to me! Maybe it is right. I don't know. I'd never really thought of it as a rule before.

Dave: You'll probably need to reflect some more on that. If that were a rule that you apply to your life, is it really true or is it just another thought, true in some circumstances and not in others?

Eva: It's certainly not always true for a lot of my work. I have a great team and there are lots of things that they know more about than me.

At that point, Dave drew the do-how map in Figure 8, summarizing what he had learned from Eva so far.

Dave: That exclamation mark at the fork in the road is what we call a do-how moment. The dread leads you down the lower fork, but it's also pointing out that you have a choice. So how does it feel if you imagine that you're going to give this great presentation, but you don't have to follow some rule that says you have to know more than everyone else at the conference?

Eva: It sounds like the blindingly obvious. At least, it does now. I'm not sure I saw it that way when we started this conversation. In fact, I don't feel particularly anxious about the presentation now. I need to think about this. Thanks.

Figure 8   Eva's do-how map

Eva's intention is to give a great presentation, but she is in danger of acting out of her negative emotion. She creates her own dread through the way she thinks about her presentation. She knows how to give a great presentation, but she doesn't recognize that the dread she feels points to the opportunity for a breakthrough. Her hidden rule of always having to know more than everyone else is driving her unconsciously to focus on what she *doesn't* want, and this is what creates the dread. By recognizing that she knows her stuff, she can relax and give a better presentation.

Later in the same program, Dave spent some time coaching Eva to make sure she had a way of recognizing the emotional triggers that led to the downward fork as they happened, as well as being able to bring to mind her positive vision of herself giving a great presentation when she needed it. He met her again a month later, after her presentation. Even before he entered her office, her PA said, "I don't know what you've done to Eva but she's like a different woman, she seems so much more relaxed." Eva herself said that the insights she gained in that session had changed her outlook about the whole way she worked, not only how she gave presentations.

The challenge is to recognize emotions for what they are. We can learn a great deal from our negative emotions – the fact that we are bothered by a sensation, or a situation – if we are simply willing to stop and look deeply at the messages they contain. This is difficult for many people.

TRY THIS: DEVELOPING AWARENESS OF YOUR DO-HOW MOMENTS

Over the next week, keep a diary of any time you notice a negative or uncomfortable emotion. It can be useful to carry around an index card in your pocket or create a list on your smartphone. Take stock before any meetings, conversations, or phone calls. You will experience emotions. Don't judge yourself for what you feel or try to make the emotion go away. The exercise is simply to notice them.

At the end of the week, go over what you have noted. Any of these moments could be a do-how moment. Is there a pattern to the emotions? Are any of them associated with opportunities to make a breakthrough?

DEVELOPING AWARENESS OF YOUR EMOTIONS

Have you ever tried to lift a car? It sounds impossible, doesn't it? And it is unless you have some leverage. With a screw jack you can easily lift your car and you may have done this to change a tire. Awareness is the leverage you need to stop and look at your emotions. Without awareness, you do not know what you are doing and what choices you are making. Indeed, without awareness you are blind to the fact that you are making choices at all. This is what was happening to the board of the investment company we described above.

We might believe that the way we behave is the way we behave and that's that; no choice is made or can be made. With awareness, we see that the opposite is true. We are faced each day with a thousand choices. Every action, every word, every thought has its impact. Consciously or unconsciously, our lives are spun out of the choices we make. Awareness is what allows us to be sensitive to our emotions and our thoughts. If we can spot those, we can lift ourselves over any barrier.

While our emotions are a powerful and accurate reporter of our hidden rules, the main challenge we face in using them is that many of us are not at all practiced at spotting our emotions. Often the time when we most need to be aware of them, when we are being swept away on a tide of emotion, is the time we are least likely to notice them. That is why it is important to develop the ability to stop and look at our own emotions, and the emotions of others around us. It is only when we spot our emotions that we create a gap in which we can choose whether to act out of emotion and habit, or out of our true intentions to achieve what is important to us.

When we ask people "How do you feel?" sometimes we get an answer reflecting the emotion that person is experiencing. However, many people have great difficulty articulating clearly and precisely what they feel. They resort to vague words like "fine," "OK," "interesting," "looking forward," or even "I think..."

Some people are more sensitive to their emotions than others, noticing the slightest breeze of emotional discomfort, while for others the emotion needs to be at gale force before it is registered. The more sensitive we are to these emotions, the sooner we spot them, and the less likely we are to be swept away by them.

Imagine you are paddling in a river. The river is shallow and barely covers your ankles. There is no chance that you will be carried away by the water flowing by. This is analogous with the normal state of affairs when our emotional current is low. Now imagine that the water level starts to rise. For whatever reason, you don't notice it rising; your attention is on something else. Pretty soon the water is up around your waist and the flow sweeps you off your feet. This is analogous to when our emotional level is high and we are thrown off balance, thrashing around in all directions at whatever has disturbed us. How much better it would be if we had noticed the level of our emotions rising. Then we would have stepped out of the river onto the bank, able to observe and wonder what the fuss was all about.

Doug told us about an argument he had had with a builder. The builder had put up an extension for him, but there were a few minor snags with the work and Doug wanted to get him back to sort them out. Despite repeated appointments, the builder failed to show up. Doug started to get more and more frustrated. What could he do? Whatever he tried, he couldn't get the builder to turn up. Following another broken appointment, Doug sat down in frustration and wrote an angry and threatening letter. If his intention was still to get the builder to put the work right, this certainly wasn't going to do the trick. He was in danger of acting out of emotion, rather than intention. This was a do-how moment.

What he had tried simply hadn't worked and he was in the grip of a negative emotion.

Luckily for Doug, his wife challenged him by asking what he thought the letter would achieve. He was able to look deeply at why he was getting so angry. He realized that his real anger was with himself for paying the builder's bill in full, and the consequent lack of power this gave him. Fortunately for Doug, he recognized the impact the letter would have before he sent it. He knew from previous experience that anger was a habitual response for him and that it rarely got him the results he wanted. He recognized his do-how moment.

There is a final twist to this story. Once Doug took the time to understand the builder better, he realized that the builder knew he ought to come back to deal with the snags, but that he feared Doug's angry response. The builder craved approval for his work, and getting angry was the very last thing that would have got him to return.

STOP, LOOK, CHOOSE

The ability to use your awareness to observe your emotions and see what they have to teach you is an essential skill, but one that few people develop naturally. We all have the capacity to witness our thoughts and feelings, but you can only notice what is there to be noticed if you take the time to stop and look. Most people have to practice doing this to develop the skill they need.

There is a very simple, three-step process that can help you develop awareness so that you can choose your behavior. When you experience any difficulty:

STOP for a moment

LOOK at your emotions and the thoughts behind them

CHOOSE how you want to respond

The first step is simply being able to *stop* and notice that there is an emotion there at all. This is more difficult than it might seem. By definition, negative emotions are something we want to avoid. The natural instinct is to do something, anything, to get away from what we are feeling. That something is very rarely helpful and usually represents the downward fork, habitual behavior or a way of thinking that has got us into the difficulty in the first place. This is what happened to Doug. He was in the grip of his anger toward the builder who had let him down, but acting out of that anger was unlikely to help him. Fortunately for Doug, his wife stopped him before he could send the letter. Most of the time we aren't so lucky. Have you ever said something that you regretted the moment you said it? That's why we need to practice this kind of stopping regularly.

When a negative emotion arises we might describe this emotion as poison, whereas in fact it is this very poison that is the medicine for our ignorance about ourselves. That is why the next step is to keep our awareness on the emotion so that we can *look* at which emotion it is and fully experience what it is telling us. This includes noticing the thoughts that lie behind the emotion. We might even recognize some physical sensations, knotting of the muscles or shallowness of breath, for example. When Doug stopped and looked, he realized that he was angry mainly because he had paid the builder in full. Just like Doug, if we stop and look at our emotional reaction, we can *choose* whether to act out of that emotion or out of a more conscious and considered intention.

STOP, LOOK, CHOOSE
When you experience
any difficulty:
STOP for a moment
LOOK at your emotions
and thoughts
CHOOSE how you
want to respond

TRY THIS: STOP, LOOK, CHOOSE

If you are not practiced at stopping and looking at your emotions and thoughts, it is unlikely that you will suddenly become mindful of them in the moments when you need to. You can start to develop this skill by regularly checking your emotions. We suggest that you take stock of your emotions each morning and evening, and also before you enter into any conversation that might prove challenging.

Sit quietly for a few moments and try to name any emotion you are experiencing. If you find yourself with a rising emotion, pause and see what the emotion is telling you. Is it fear, anger, sadness, or perhaps guilt? The more you practice spotting and naming your emotions, the easier doing so will become. Don't try to suppress the emotion, simply notice it and name it. You might hear some thoughts along with the emotion and it can be helpful to make a note of these too.

Pay particular attention to how the emotion feels in your body. Consciously scan your body from the top of the head to the soles of your feet, noticing any tension in your face, neck, shoulders, and abdomen. Relax any tension that you feel. Notice the effect the emotion has on your breathing. Breathe deeply to release the emotion. The simple act of breathing deeply can dissolve many negative emotions.

NEGATIVE EMOTIONS CONTAIN A POSITIVE MESSAGE

We sometimes get asked if it isn't negative to dwell on all these kinds of emotions. Playing to your strengths and having a positive outlook is a very important ingredient for success, and creating a positive atmosphere has an energizing effect. But no matter how positive and upbeat you are, you will come across situations that are difficult and people who frustrate you. This is especially true in times of change or when you need to make a breakthrough. Suffering and difficulty are facts of work and life. So what do you do with the negative experiences and emotions? When you feel like you are stuck in Groundhog Day, you need to turn and face your discomfort and see it for what it is, a signpost to a breakthrough.

All emotions are there for a reason; ironically, the more we try to avoid the message they want to deliver, the more hold they have over us. Negative emotions contain a positive message if we take the time to listen. It is when we really get in touch with the emotion that it loses its hold over us and we have more freedom to choose. By facing your discomfort, you can spot the do-how moments when your choices make a difference. By simply sitting with the emotion rather than reacting out of it, you can step beyond the self-limitation that it points to, and what bothers you can become an opportunity to make a breakthrough.

> **When we get in touch with an emotion it loses its hold over us and we have more freedom to choose**

MINDFULNESS

The ability to stop and simply observe the flow of thoughts, feelings, and physical sensations is usually called mindfulness. It is a very powerful way to develop awareness. It has many other spinoff benefits, such as increased motivation, empathy, and resilience, along with lower levels of stress and increased creativity and energy. In fact, many large organizations, including Google, Sony, Carlsberg, GE Healthcare, the US Army, and the British National Health Service, teach some kind of mindfulness practice to many of their staff. To experience why this is important, try the short exercise below.

> **TRY THIS**: THE BARREL FULL OF MONKEYS
> Put down anything you are holding, sit comfortably, if possible close your eyes, and stay silent for one minute. Make a note of what you noticed.

People report many different things when they try this experiment. They might have noticed that they were thinking about what to have for dinner, or remembering what had happened earlier that day. They might have noticed some anxiety about something they have to do or anticipation about meeting someone that evening. They might just have noticed an ache somewhere in their body, or the noise of a computer. The key point is that we always notice something, and often it's something we simply haven't recognized before.

It isn't that sensations suddenly appear the moment we become silent; far from it. Our mind is like a barrel full of monkeys. A constant stream of thoughts, feelings, imaginings, and emotions flows through it all the time, we just aren't aware of it. And even though these thoughts and feelings elude our attention, they still have an impact on us. Have you ever snapped at someone, and only afterward realized that they were receiving the sharp outcome of some unexplained anxiety at the back of your mind?

Perhaps you have been lying in bed at night and heard the tick of your watch or a clock. You may have had the same watch on your wrist all day and never noticed it tick, yet in the quiet of the night the tick is quite audible. And it is in the silence that we finally hear what makes us tick. This is why mindfulness practice can be uncomfortable for some people. We instinctively know that we will be confronted with what we'd rather not face – our hidden and unconscious self.

If you have ever used a walkie-talkie, you will know that they have two modes of operation: transmit and receive. When you want to transmit you press a button. When you want to receive you let go of the button. What is important to know, if you want to communicate with the other person, is that you can't receive when you are on transmit. It's also like that with the development of your awareness. If you never listen, if you never let go of the transmit button, you will not and cannot notice what is there to be seen and heard. That is why learning to regularly stop and look at our emotions is important. You can strengthen your mindfulness further with a very simple practice.

TRY THIS: STRENGTHENING MINDFULNESS

As before, sit in silence and watch your thoughts for one minute. This time, place your awareness on your breath, as you draw it in and then let it out again. Find the physical sensation of your breath in your body. For some people this is the feeling of air passing over their nostrils, for others it is the sense of their abdomen rising and falling. Just make sure that you are noticing a physical sensation, not a thought or idea. Don't try to control your breath, simply find the physical sensation of it as it goes in and out and observe it. Count "one" on the in-breath, "two" on the out-breath, "three" on the next in-breath, and so on. When you reach the count of ten, start at one again. Try keeping silent for three minutes, or even longer if you prefer.

So what happened?

Did you count all the way to ten then start again? If you did this for three minutes, well done! Most people find that they get distracted before they reach ten. Something comes up in the mind and they follow that thought. Their breathing keeps going, of course, but their awareness has wandered off elsewhere. One of the best comments we have ever heard after this exercise was: "I did really well that time. I got all the way to sixteen before my attention wandered!"

This practice develops the capacity to concentrate your awareness. If an interesting thought arises, simply ignore it and keep your awareness on your breath. The aim is not to stop thinking, simply to let thoughts pass by and not allow yourself to be distracted by them. Even if what seems like a great insight arises, just let it go. Keep your awareness focused on your breathing.

Think of awareness as a young puppy at its first obedience class. You place it a few yards away and tell it to stay. You turn your back, and after a few seconds the puppy has wandered off. That's what our awareness is like. If you want to develop self-awareness, you need to train your awareness to stay in one place. Only if you can do that can you have any hope of using that awareness to look closely at what's really going on inside you.

If you are really serious about developing your awareness, we recommend that you do at least 20 minutes of awareness practice twice a day. However, even 2 minutes twice a day will yield significant benefits and lead to insights and greater self-awareness. If you do just one thing as a result of reading this book, we hope it is this. Simply find 2 minutes in the morning and 2 minutes in the afternoon or early evening and sit in silence, following your breath. Notice how you feel and notice that you have the freedom to choose how you respond.

A REFUGE FROM THE RIVER OF THOUGHTS

Following your breath in this way is a refuge from the river of thoughts, sensations, feelings, and imaginations that continually flows through your field of attention. Suppose that you are in this river and you simply want to stand in one place to observe what happens at that spot. However, this is very difficult. The flow of the river keeps on sweeping you off your feet and taking you downstream. If left to its own devices, your untrained awareness, which is not strong enough or disciplined enough to stay in one place, will be continuously swept away by the flow of your thoughts.

Suppose now that there is a rock in the river that you can climb onto. You can quite happily sit there and watch the water going by. In our analogy, our breath is the rock, which we use to keep our awareness in one place, while our thoughts, sensations, feelings, and imaginations are the river. Every so often, we still get swept away by some particularly attractive thought, but when we realize that has happened, we just climb out onto the rock of our breath again.

Awareness is just like any other capacity. The more you exercise it, the stronger it gets. The good news is that even a small amount of practice every day will gradually develop your ability. The key is to exercise regularly, though. If you only try to practice when you need it, the capacity simply won't be adequately developed.

Awareness is just like any other capacity – the more you exercise it, the stronger it gets

The Zen Master and writer Thich Nhat Hanh tells a story that illustrates this point. He once lived in a small house in France, the kind with wooden shutters. He had lived there for a few months, working on a new book. He had papers all around the room where he was working. One morning, he noticed a storm in the distance and realized that it was headed toward him and his little house. He ran outside to close the shutters, but found that the hinges were all rusted and he could not get them closed. He worked away at loosening the hinges, but couldn't loosen up the shutters in time. When the storm hit, the wind and rain tore through the house, blowing papers all over the place. It took him several days to reassemble them and even then, some were missing or ruined. He realized that he needed to be prepared, and that the time to repair shutters is not minutes before a storm hits. The whole experience strengthened his awareness.

DON'T JUST DO SOMETHING, SIT THERE!

We have talked in this chapter about the importance of emotions, particularly negative emotions, as feedback. If you do the awareness practice that we suggest above, you will find that you gradually develop the control to start looking deeply at all the emotions and thoughts that determine so much of your behavior. You will probably become more sensitive to the emotions of others around you, too. In any case, no matter how sensitive or insensitive you are to your emotions, there will be occasions when you become aware that something is bothering you. This is feedback that something is happening to take you outside the comfort zone defined by your hidden rules. These are precious moments, when you are being invited to take stock. The only sensible advice for those moments is: "Don't just do something, sit there!" In other words, whatever course of action you are embarked on, pause and reflect on what is really going on. Is your behavior going to be helpful, or is it merely your habitual response, driven by your hidden rules? Only then do you choose. Choose your behavior, rather than your behavior choosing you. Choose to act in a way that will be useful and productive. Choose to let go of acting out of emotion, out of your habitual way of responding. Choose to see yourself and your motivations as they really are and to step above them. You can run away from your difficulties or repress them, but they are still there. If you have the courage to stop and look, whatever bothers you can lead to a breakthrough.

> **If you have the courage to stop and look, whatever bothers you can lead to a breakthrough**

TRY THIS: FROM BOTHER TO BREAKTHROUGH

Think of a situation in which you currently experience a negative or afflictive emotion. This might be a situation where you feel stuck or where you need a breakthrough. Try to choose something that reflects any patterns there are to the difficulties you face.

Find somewhere quiet where you can look deeply into the emotion you are experiencing.

Start by simply following your breath in the way we describe in this chapter. Do this for a few minutes and just let any thoughts go by.

Next, bring to mind the situation that is bothering you and allow yourself to experience the emotion. Feel how the emotion is held in your body, perhaps as a shortening of the breath or a tightening of the muscles in the face, shoulders, or abdomen. Scan your body from the crown of your head to the soles of your feet, noticing any subtle ways in which the emotion is held in your body. Let go of any tension.

Now name the emotion. Was it fear, anger, sadness, or some other emotion?

Notice any thoughts associated with the emotion, especially thoughts about what you or others should or shouldn't do.

Finish by following your breath for a few more minutes, just letting any thoughts pass. Take a few deep, slow, long breaths deep down into your abdomen.

Chapter 5

PICTURE THE POSITIVE, PRECISE POSSIBILITY

How to spell out the breakthrough you want

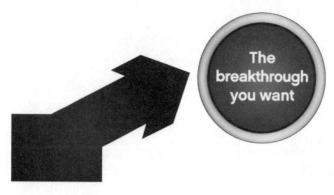

The breakthrough you want

Do you remember the Spice Girls? In 1996 you would have to have been on another planet to avoid Posh, Scary, Baby, Sporty, and Ginger Spice declaring to the world "I'll tell you what I want, what I really, really want." They really knew what they wanted and, judging by their success over the following years, they really, really got it.

Knowing what you want is a key part of making change happen. When you know what you want, you have the choice to live from a vision of what is possible rather than out of your limitations. It's not enough to have a vague idea of what you want, though. You need to spell it out in a way that makes the alternative to your habitual response vivid and compelling. The more difficult the change you want to make, the bigger and bolder your declaration of what you want needs to be. Your breakthrough must grab your attention when you reach that fork in the road where your choices matter most.

We have the choice to live from a vision of what is possible rather than out of our limitations

TWO PARTS TO CHANGE

There are two things you need to clarify for any change you want to make. The first part is the overall outcome or result that you want. For example, one of our clients, a politician called Will, had major plans for the city where he lived and worked and wanted to build the commitment of the most influential people there to his plan. The first thing he had to do was to spell out precisely what that meant. How would he know that he had their commitment and what would happen as a result? We'll say more about that later, but at this stage it's enough to recognize that Will had some thinking to do to make sure that his goal was clear.

There's also a second part, and that's what we're interested in here. You need to spell out what you want to change about how you think and behave. It's when you get to grips with your role in creating the outcome you want that you're on the road from know-how to do-how. We worked with Will on this, because he wasn't happy with the progress he had made so far. Something about his behavior simply wasn't aligned with his goal and he had the insight to see this and the courage to admit it. He worked hard to understand what sort of person he needed to be to win the commitment he wanted from the decision makers in his city. How did he want to conduct himself, what behavior did he need to exhibit to be consistent with his goal?

This gives us two different parts within one breakthrough. The first is the overall outcome or result that you want. The second is a goal for how you want to respond, how you want to think and behave to give yourself the best shot at achieving the result you want. This is the breakthrough that we want to spell out in this chapter, although everything we say is equally applicable to defining the overall outcome or result that you want to achieve. Figure 9 shows how the two parts relate to each other.

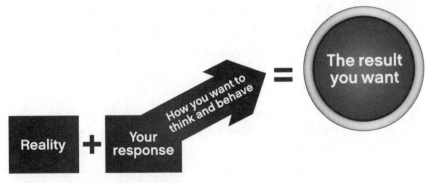

Figure 9   Two kinds of breakthrough

SOMETHING HAS TO MATTER

We were once invited to watch a soccer match between Shrewsbury Town and Cheltenham in the English League Two, the fourth-highest division overall. The quality of the football left a lot to be desired, but what really struck us was the commitment of the fans, particularly the 100 or so away fans. Why would anyone travel halfway across the country on a wet Tuesday in March to watch two lower-league sides? We don't know the answer to that question, but we do know that attending mattered to them more than the ordeal of spending most of the evening on a coach and then sitting on a cold and windy terrace.

While putting up with the discomfort required to make a breakthrough may seem a lot to ask – and it is – it's difficult to step beyond the limits of your hidden rules unless something matters more to you than your own comfort. Without the energy that comes when there is something significant at stake, you will give up. That is why big, bold goals are better than little, meek goals. Whatever you commit to, make sure that it's about something more than a self-centered agenda. In our experience, this is something that great leaders understand very well. They establish a worthwhile vision bigger than themselves that people can buy into.

TRY THIS: YOUR BREAKTHROUGH

What is the overall outcome or result that you want to achieve? Write it down. Make sure it's something that matters to you, something that you're willing to work for.

What do you want to change about the way you think and behave? How do you need to change so that your behavior is aligned with your overall goal? Write that down as well.

THE FOUR PS
In our experience, there are four things that really help when spelling out the breakthrough you want to make. These are:

Picture the breakthrough you want to make

State the breakthrough in **positive** terms

Be **precise** about what the breakthrough looks, sounds, and feels like

Look beyond the problems – if anything were **possible**, what would you want to make possible?

We call these the four Ps. When you spell out the breakthrough, you are defining the positive, precise possibility for how you want things to be. By doing this you can help ensure that your future will be guided by where you are heading rather than where you have come from.

PICTURE THE BREAKTHROUGH
What you imagine the world can be, it can become. Whatever change you want to make, there is a way of achieving it if you allow yourself to step outside the limits of your hidden rules and choose a way of responding that is more appropriate. The pictures you create in your mind have a big impact on your behavior, so if you can picture what you are trying to achieve, you can make it a reality.

It is important to have a clear image of what success looks like. This picture has to be strong enough and clear enough to displace the equivalent picture that triggers your habitual behavior. We don't only mean a visual representation – picturing the breakthrough you want to make might also include a soundtrack and moving images. Different people tap into different senses, including sight, sound, touch, or movement, and even smell and taste. The stronger your image of what you want, the stronger it becomes as an alternative to your habitual responses.

One of our clients, a senior police officer, is regarded by his colleagues as something of a miracle worker. He seems to be able to find his way through the tangle of bureaucracy to make things happen that his colleagues can only dream of. He has an incredibly positive and enthusiastic outlook on life. Everyone loves working with him and we wondered whether that was a big component of his success. We asked him what he does that makes him so effective. He told us that he imagines himself as one of the contestants from the television show *Gladiators*, knocking all obstacles aside. This image makes sense. He is unstoppable but also fun to be around. He never lets anything get in his way, but he also never takes anything too seriously or becomes aggressive.

Any breakthrough begins with an act of imagination

Any breakthrough begins with an act of imagination. Being able to imagine how you want things to be is a key component of making the breakthrough a reality. When we asked Will what he visualized when he thought about his vision for the city, he had a clear picture in his mind. He said that he saw all the key players working together with one plan. It didn't have to be *his* plan, but there was just one plan that everyone supported with action. He imagined looking out over the city and seeing cranes in the sky, representing some of the major developments that had stalled over the past decade due to infighting but were now, in his picture of success, under construction.

TRY THIS: WHO WILL YOU BECOME?

Find somewhere quiet and relaxing to do this exercise. Sit comfortably and close your eyes. Imagine that you are in one of your favorite places, sitting quietly and relaxing.

Now imagine that you are joined by another person. That person is you from 15 years ago. (You can adjust the timescale if it is inappropriate.)

What do you notice about your younger self? What
do they notice about you? What advice do they offer
you? What advice would you offer them? Can you
see the roots of your current self in that self from 15
years ago?

Your younger self now leaves and you are alone
again with your thoughts.

After some time, you are joined by another person.
Now this is you in 15 years' time.

What do you notice about your older self? What do
they notice about you? What advice do they offer
you? What advice would you offer them? Can you
see the roots of your future self in your own current
commitments and qualities?

Your older self now leaves and you are alone again
with your thoughts. Make a note of any insights that
this visualization brings for you.

FIND A ROLE MODEL

We met a woman some years ago who shared in a workshop that she
lacked confidence. She explained that she didn't know how to "do"
confidence. The irony was that she was a university drama teacher
and knew how to act confidently when on stage. We worked with
her to draw out what she was calling on when she played a part that
required her to portray confidence. She realized that she had a strong
image of her sister as a bold and self-assured woman and that was
what she drew on when she acted a part that required her to appear
confident. Once she spotted this ability to draw on her sister as a role
model, it was enough to help her make a breakthrough that stayed
with her.

You can find a positive picture that can help you make a breakthrough with any of your rules by looking at the merits of the opposite. For example, Fran has a rule that she must "avoid criticism." She can examine the rule by asking herself if there is ever any merit in being criticized, such as learning from feedback, identifying areas for development, and so on. She can then picture these positive benefits and imagine what she would need to do to create them. If she finds role models who demonstrate the success of rules different from her own and looks carefully at how they behave, she will learn from them.

Looking for role models who are already doing what you want to learn to do is a very worthwhile activity. Seeing someone who has the do-how you need in action is the best way of creating a mental image of that behavior in practice. If Fran looks for someone who finds it beneficial to invite criticism (although filtered through their rules they would probably call it getting useful feedback), she would see how to do this skillfully.

TRY THIS: **FIND YOUR ROLE MODEL**

Who do you know who is a role model of the behavior that you want to exhibit? Observe them carefully. What do they say? What is their body language? Listen to them speak and see whether you can identify any ways of thinking that can help you. Ask if you can meet and talk with them and see what insights you gain.

Imagine that you were asked to act the part of that person in a play. What are their essential characteristics? Don't focus too much on mannerisms, but try to get at what is going on inside. What are their thoughts?

PRACTICE MAKES PERFECT

There is a wonderful story about the American golfer Arnold Palmer, who was being interviewed following a successful tournament. The interviewer asked him the secret of his success. Palmer answered, "I guess I'm just lucky." The interviewer enquired, "But doesn't the fact that you practice several hours every day have something to do with your success?" Palmer looked slightly puzzled. "Well, the funny thing is, the more I practice, the luckier I get!"

It may seem too obvious to say, but practice really does makes perfect. Whatever breakthrough you want to make, you need to practice thinking and behaving in a way that is consistent with that breakthrough.

Find simple and safe places to practice. You wouldn't start your first driving lesson in a Formula 1 car and you don't need to practice whatever skill you want to develop in the most challenging and difficult situation. If you want to get better at giving people difficult feedback, start with someone you have a good relationship with and tell them that you want to practice. You'll discover more from this than any amount of thinking and planning, and what you learn will make it easier to picture the breakthrough you want.

In an organizational change program, giving people safe places to practice will do more than any number of posters or screensavers reminding them of the corporate values. Staff will learn more from trying and sometimes failing than from any other activity.

VISUALIZE AND AFFIRM THE BREAKTHROUGH

It is helpful to explicitly affirm and visualize the positive way of behaving that would be more helpful to you than your existing habitual response. If it helps you, talk to yourself about what you see. There is a reason that top tennis players mutter away to themselves as they face their opponents. Positive self-talk is a great way of creating a helpful state of mind and displacing unhelpful thoughts.

TRY THIS: VISUALIZE AND AFFIRM YOUR BREAKTHROUGH

Find somewhere quiet and relaxing to do this exercise. Sit comfortably and close your eyes. Create a mental image of yourself successfully making the breakthrough that you want. What does it look like? What do you see? What will you feel like once you have made the breakthrough?

What words sum up the breakthrough you want to make? Imagine that you are your own cheerleader or coach and find a form of words or slogan that you find encouraging.

What did you learn from this exercise? Does this change what you wrote earlier about your breakthrough?

STATE THE BREAKTHROUGH IN **POSITIVE** TERMS

Have you ever put batteries into a new torch or camera? If you put them in the right way around, you get power and everything works. If you put them in the wrong way around, the device doesn't operate and you may even do some damage. Similarly, if you put your own batteries in the wrong way around – having negative intentions, for example – you can lose your motivation and feel powerless to make a breakthrough.

Playing to win is not the same as playing not to lose. Just watch a football match where both teams are playing not to lose and you'll soon see the difference. However, when you get your intentions lined up in the positive direction so that you are clear what you want, you will feel energized and be in a much stronger position to make positive choices when the time comes.

By positive intentions, we mean what you are drawn to and what you want to create and offer to the world. Positive intentions are associated with the things that you love and are excited about. On the other hand, there are intentions about avoiding what is bad, what to stay away from or avoid, what you need from the world in order to be happy. These negative intentions are associated with what you fear or don't want to lose. When you are stuck, it is often because you are hooked on a negative intention. You might think that it's quite simple to state what you want. So it is, but in our experience it's far from common for people to be clear about what they want, especially when they are stuck. Eva in the previous chapter doesn't want to look stupid; Tom the trainer doesn't want his trainees to feel uncomfortable. These are both negative intentions.

Playing to win is not the same as playing not to lose

The more positive you are about what you want, the more likely you are to have the motivation and energy to make it happen and the more likely you are to achieve it. However, because of the way your hidden rules drive your behavior, if all you have is a vague idea of what you *don't* want, perversely, you will tend to get what you don't want. This might seem contradictory, but it is easy to see how these two statements are both true.

Knowing what you don't want is not the same as knowing what you want. They look the same semantically, but they are polar opposites when it comes to the effect they have on your thoughts, emotions, and behavior. Take the example of Eva with her fear of public speaking. She is almost entirely focused on what she *doesn't* want, which is to dry up and give a poor presentation. Because of this, she is filled with anxiety and dread, which causes her to dry up. It leads to the very thing she is trying to avoid. However, when she starts to focus her attention on what she wants in a positive way, she begins to see the possibility that she can deliver a great presentation. Focusing on what she wants helps her relax when she realizes that she knows what it looks and feels like to be good at public speaking.

Simon is an example of someone who discovered the importance of this kind of positive thinking. Like many middle managers, he considered himself to be overworked and underpaid. When we met him he was worn out from running a project for an electrical generation equipment company, coordinating two teams, a manufacturing team in Texas and an installation crew in England. Anyone listening to Simon for more than a few minutes could see the pressure he was under and it wasn't difficult to hear that his main goal was to "avoid doing a bad job." He had suffered a few setbacks, including some faulty equipment that should have been checked before it left the plant but that had been delivered to the construction site and delayed the whole project for several months. The client wasn't happy and neither was Simon's boss. Simon was fearful that he would lose his job if he didn't get the project back on track again.

From this mindset, it was difficult for Simon to feel positively motivated and he was anxious most of the time. He told us that he spent sleepless nights mentally rehearsing any further difficulties that might arise. It was easy to see how this drained his energy. His only solace, he told us, was that some other aspects of the project were also in difficulty and he felt relief that he wasn't doing as poorly as some of his colleagues. He had started to measure his success by how badly he was doing rather than how well.

You might think that this is an extreme example, but most people have some negative goals, at least unconsciously. They may cover up their fears with positive language, but their inner dialogue is almost entirely negative. It's then an uphill struggle to deliver good results.

We worked with Simon to help him uncover this energy-sapping internal chatter. We also assisted him in clarifying what energized him, what had excited him in the first place and led him to a career in energy generation. He talked about the thrill he got out of being around big construction projects. He developed a positive message for himself about what it meant to do a great job, to bring together multiple strands of people, materials, and equipment and weave them together at the right place and the right time to create a generating plant with enough power to light up Dallas or Derby.

Simon started to notice opportunities to improve the way the project was organized and he got excited about the opportunity to implement some of these ideas. His team said that he became more open to their ideas too and he gave them more positive feedback when things went well. His boss could see the difference in him and his team were more motivated, with more ideas and energy to improve what they were doing. By focusing on a positive goal, Simon turned a stressful situation that was going from bad to worse into one of the most exciting projects he had ever experienced.

We have witnessed many people come alive simply by helping them focus on what they want rather than what they don't want. Can you imagine what the outcome would have been if Martin Luther King had started his "I have a dream" speech with "There's a big problem with racism"? He set out what he wanted, not what he didn't want. Or think about Winston Churchill's stirring "We shall fight them on the beaches." Would that speech still be remembered if he had muttered on about not wanting to lose the war?

There are two main reasons for positive statements of what you want being more effective than negative statements of what you don't want. First, as we can see from the examples above, stating the breakthrough that you want to make in a positive way taps into emotions that are motivating. In contrast, focusing on what you don't want arouses negative emotions, which are demotivating and can only sap your energy.

Secondly, the brain simply doesn't process negatives at the unconscious level. This has been shown time and time again in various devious and clever ways by psychologists. We remember one occasion when we were having dinner with some clients. One of their colleagues, Dean, had gone to hospital that day for a minor operation, which involved scraping the surface of the eye to remove the layer of tissue on the cornea. Dean had explained in gory detail at a previous meeting what was involved and, although it was a relatively simple procedure, it did sound excruciating. Someone happened to say, "Best not to think about what's happening to Dean just now." Of course, everyone immediately thought of exactly what was

Thinking about what you *don't* want leads you to what you don't want – focusing on what you want leads to a breakthrough

happening to Dean and several of us winced. The mere mention of him was enough to bring the whole procedure to mind and the "best not to" part of the suggestion didn't make the slightest difference. Anyone who has told a child "don't go near that muddy puddle" also knows this effect, usually only succeeding in letting the child know that there is a muddy puddle nearby.

This situation occurs largely because of the way our mind works. We communicate in words, but the mind creates an internal representation of the words using whatever senses we prefer. When we hear the words we create images and experience physical feelings in the body, along with internal dialogue fired off by associations with what we have heard. We summarize this entire experience as our "state."

THE IMPORTANCE OF STATE

We want to emphasize the importance of your emotional and physical state in making change happen. If you really want to bring your break-through to life, you need to create as vivid and precise a representation as possible of the state you need in order to achieve that breakthrough. In the example of Eva, she could make rapid progress because she had already experienced what it was like to give a good presentation in a relaxed state. She could access this experience to create a precise rep-resentation of how her breakthrough would look, sound, and feel.

Nothing happens without motivation and that means having access to useful emotional states. When you are stuck, it is often because you are focusing on what you don't want, which leads to a negative emotional state that is inherently demotivating. There are, of course, situations in which avoiding what you don't want can be truly energizing, as you will know if you have ever been confronted by a snarling dog. In such cases, the fear provides you with exactly the right response and you don't feel stuck or powerless – you run like crazy or face the dog down. In most cases, however, the breakthrough needs to be something that you asso-ciate with a positive state, something you feel excited and energized by. Without this, change is rarely possible.

If there is a negative thought you want to drop, it can be helpful to identify the "antidote" to it. By antidote, we mean the positive thought that would be helpful for you in achieving your breakthrough. It is useful to think of specific situations where using positive self-talk will help you most. Eva was filled with dread when giving a big presentation because of her thoughts "the audience will judge me" and "I'll dry up and won't know what to say." She identified "the audience will love what I have to say" and "I know my stuff" as antidote thoughts that helped her access the right state to give the presentation. She would consciously fill her mind with these thoughts for the few hours before she spoke. Many sportspeople use this approach – think of Muhammad Ali's mantra "I am the greatest."

One starting point for this is to ask yourself: "What is the antidote to the aspect of my rules that is holding me back?" For example, if you have a nagging idea that you are not good enough and need to avoid criticism, then tell yourself that you *are* good enough and that feedback can help you be even better. Visualize what it means to be good enough. Think through how you will behave when you know that you are good enough and practice behaving that way.

TRY THIS: POSITIVE SELF-TALK

What positive self-talk would be useful for you? Is there a thought that you want to drop? What is the antidote to that thought? In what situations would positive self-talk help you most?

Practice this positive self-talk over the next few days and weeks. What happens? What did you learn?

Will, the politician we mentioned earlier in this chapter, shared with us that his habit was to decide what was needed and get swiftly into action. He would become frustrated by all the bickering and jockeying for position that got in the way of progress and couldn't understand why people didn't simply come together for the common good of the city. He would sometimes openly show his anger and disappointment at the way other people behaved and this ran counter to his goal of gaining the commitment and support of those who were influential. He found himself thinking, "I don't want to have to deal with people who aren't as committed to this as I am." This is a negative intention and it was holding him back. He worked at this and his mantra became: "I want to share my commitment to this city." This simple shift in thinking had a dramatic effect. He created a short presentation setting out a vision for the city. Wherever he went, he found an opportunity to share this vision and communicate his personal commitment. He stopped judging other people's lack of vision and found that his presentation became the "grit in the oyster." All kinds of ideas and plans began to coalesce around that simple starting point. He had made a breakthrough.

TRY THIS: YOUR POSITIVE BREAKTHROUGH

Look at the breakthrough that you wrote down earlier. Is there anything in it that is negative? Look for words such as "I don't want..." or "I want to avoid..." or "There will be less..." Sometimes the negative language can be more subtle. The key is to be honest: Is the breakthrough about something you want and feel positive toward, or is it about something you don't want and feel negative about?

Try rewriting your breakthrough so that it is entirely positive. It can help to talk this through with a friend. You can get stuck in ways of thinking so that you can't see a way of stating what you want positively.

BE **PRECISE** ABOUT WHAT THE BREAKTHROUGH LOOKS, SOUNDS, AND FEELS LIKE

The more precise you are, the easier it is to change. We could just leave this section at that, but if you are really paying attention to what we are saying you might be asking a number of questions, such as:

Who do you mean by "you"?

Precise about what?

Easier in what way?

Change what, exactly?

These questions illustrate that in the normal use of language we leave a lot of detail to be filled in by the context or the reader's imagination. This is fine most of the time, but if we want to give ourselves the best possible chance of making a breakthrough, it really helps to spell out all the details. The full sentence, if we fill in all the blanks, becomes something like:

> **The more precise you** (the person trying to make a breakthrough) **are** (about the details of the behavior described in terms of what you would do, what you would think, and what you would feel like, plus any other details that are important to describe fully the total physical and emotional state related to that behavior you want to adopt in order to make a breakthrough), **the easier it is** (or will be) **to** (spot opportunities to behave in that way and choose to behave that way when you experience a negative emotion that would normally prompt you to behave in a way that does not get you the results you want in those situations where you currently feel stuck and are not getting the results you want, so that by choosing a different behavior you can) **change** (the result of your interaction).

That's quite a mouthful and we don't suggest that you try to communicate this way unless you want to sound like you've swallowed a legal dictionary. However, there is an important point in all of this.

Language is powerfully hypnotic. By hypnotic in this context we mean that it can alter our state of mind and plant in it ideas of which we are not fully aware. That is the last thing we need when we are wrestling with hidden rules operating at an unconscious level. And the more vague the language, the more hypnotic it can be.

Our mind is a meaning-making machine that eagerly and creatively fills in any gaps with whatever happens to be swirling around at the time. Advertisers, politicians, and marketing people all love vague language, which does have a role when we want to persuade or encourage. It wouldn't have helped for Winston Churchill to have spelled out precisely which beaches we were going to fight on, with whom, and with what weapons, for example. Nevertheless, it is useful to recognize that when a politician says "vote for change," each of us fills in the blanks with whatever is most important to us. "Change what precisely?" you might ask – but few of us do.

Hypnotic language is about suggestion. Some years ago there was a popular practice for energy companies to ring people at home and ask, "Would you like to save money on your energy bill?" Very few people would disagree with that suggestion, but what the caller failed to define was precisely how much (or how little) you would save and at what cost in terms of inconvenience. So there are many situations and professions where vague language is of value, but when it comes to making a breakthrough it is better to use precise language to describe what you want.

Ken has a goal to be a "better director." Suppose that we followed him around with a video camera for a month. Would we ever see him being a better director? If we showed the video to a hundred people and asked them what they saw, do you think any of them would say, "We saw a guy called Ken being a better director"? Someone might say that they saw Ken talk to people or set people goals or reprimand people or praise people, but it's very unlikely that they would describe his behavior as being a better director, unless we, and more importantly Ken, answer the question: "Better in what way precisely?" If we asked ten people what it means to be a better director, we would get at least ten different answers. Those answers might be useful as a general guide, but you can be pretty sure that they won't quite hit the mark for Ken.

Another possibility is simply to ask Ken what it would *look like* if he were a better director, or if he can give an example of what it *means* to be a better director. He might reply in all sorts of ways, but let's suppose that he says it means that he wants to improve his delegation skills. That is a little more precise, but it still leaves a lot to the imagination. For one person improved delegation might mean passing specific tasks on to others; to another person it could mean remembering to hold people to account for tasks that have been delegated to them. We need to find out from Ken whether he has a clear picture of what this looks like. If we wanted Ken to act out "improved delegation," would he know what to do?

The best place to find the precise definition we are looking for is in Ken's own experience. He may well have experience of delegating well in other circumstances, in which case we can explore with him what he did, what he thought, and what he felt. Even if he doesn't have that experience himself, he may have in mind other people he sees as delegating skillfully. He can use his knowledge of those role models to enquire how precisely they do delegation and even how they think and feel.

> **Precise language breaks the hypnotic illusion that we know what is really meant by what is being said**

Where we want to get to with Ken is a kind of mental movie so that he knows precisely what to do when his do-how moment comes. We often ask clients to role-play with us what their breakthrough would look like. This is by far the best way to check that there is a precise understanding that can easily be accessed.

PRECISE LANGUAGE

Precise language breaks the hypnotic illusion that we know what is really meant by what is being said. One technique that is very powerful is to listen carefully to what is being said, particularly for any gaps that have to be filled in by the imagination, and to invite the person speaking to fill in those gaps.

We were once asked to deliver some team building for a large local authority, the body responsible for local government. Local authorities in the United Kingdom usually have a senior management team comprising the chief executive and the directors responsible for delivery of services. They also, but not always, have a cabinet made up of the political leader of the council and the most senior council members. In this particular local authority they came together every two weeks in what was called the council management team. We attended a meeting with the deputy chief executive, Lee, to clarify the precise goal for the work. We were told that the purpose of the event was to improve communication. The words "improve communication" are probably as vague as it gets in the English language and so we asked the obvious questions: improve in what way, communication between whom, about what?

By simply focusing on Lee's replies and continually inviting her to clarify any vagueness or ambiguity, we worked our way through to a very different goal. We discovered that a major rift had opened up between the chief executive and the council leader. The two of them had ended up having an open shouting match in the presence of partners from the city, a state of affairs that threatened to destabilize the whole organization. The real goal we identified was to get the two of them talking to each other in a civil manner. Lee had understandably shown some considerable discomfort and she was reluctant to discuss the situation openly. By using the power of precise language, we were able to get to the root of the issue and design an intervention that led to a breakthrough.

The key to being precise in describing your breakthrough is to refuse to accept anything but what is explicitly spelt out. In other words, don't fill in the blanks using your imagination, but work hard to make the breakthrough explicit, precise, and concise. Ask what, who, when, where, why, and how precisely. For example, "I want to be a better listener" might be an important goal for you. But better in what way, listening to whom, when, in what circumstances? These are just some of the gaps that it might be important to fill. "Better at listening to people I don't agree with" might be more precise, or "Being able to take a genuine interest in a customer's grievances even when they are rude and angry" might be the breakthrough that you really want to make.

TRY THIS: WHAT PRECISELY IS THE BREAKTHROUGH YOU WANT?

Take a look at the breakthrough you wrote down earlier. Can you be more precise in what you are saying?

What are the gaps that someone reading your breakthrough would have to fill with their imagination or make assumptions about?

IF ANYTHING WERE **POSSIBLE**, WHAT WOULD YOU WANT TO MAKE POSSIBLE?

To paraphrase Henry Ford, whether you believe you can or you believe you can't, you are probably right. The greatest limit you can put on what you can achieve is failing to use your imagination to see what might be possible if you put your mind to it. Learning to see the possibility of a breakthrough is sometimes the biggest breakthrough you can make, particularly when you are deeply stuck and all you can see are the problems that surround you.

There are two ways to think about a breakthrough. The first is to imagine what the situation would be like if your problems were fixed. If you have a critical boss, you might see it as a breakthrough if she stops criticizing you. You could take this idea and examine it so that you can state it more positively. Perhaps what you really want is for her to give you some positive feedback or to let you get on with your work. That would be a good starting point to move the conversation on to what you personally can do to change things, although it's still limited. The basic premise for the breakthrough is rooted in the way things are now, in the problem. However you phrase things, you are still really dealing with fixing your difficulties. That's not a bad thing, merely limited. It's like trying to fix a problem concerning a typewriter. You'll end up with a better typewriter, but you won't invent the computer.

There is a more powerful way: ask yourself what you really want. The chances are that you will edit your answer based on what you think is possible starting from the point of fixing the problems that you have right now. In other words, if you have a typewriter, you will say that you want a better typewriter rather than allowing yourself to imagine a machine with the capabilities of a modern computer. To quote Henry Ford again, he once said that if he had asked his customers what they wanted they would have replied "a faster horse." So ask yourself again, what do you really want?

ALF'S ONE-HOUR SAUSAGES

This simple act of allowing yourself to imagine what might be possible and what the breakthrough might look like can itself lead to that breakthrough becoming more possible. We were once asked to work with Chris, a senior manager from a large producer of sausages. He was responsible for a team tasked with minimizing waste from the plant and we had been asked by the production director to help him identify a breakthrough that the team could work on. The team had already delivered hundreds of thousands of pounds in annual savings by eliminating waste from the manufacturing process, and as a beneficial spinoff they had reduced lead times for manufacturing the sausages from five days to four days from raw materials to sausages delivered to the supermarket door. This was already better than the industry average and Chris resisted the idea that they needed to set new goals, as he saw the team as successful. We asked him what would represent a breakthrough, but he didn't think that a breakthrough was possible. The team had a range of initiatives planned and he felt that little further progress was to be had. He talked us through the impressive list of changes the team had implemented and how these had made a significant difference to the company's bottom line.

We changed tack and asked him what the most significant challenges were that the organization faced. He became much more energized at that point. They were running out of space to expand on their urban site, close to the center of a large city. They were also getting pressure from their largest customers, the major supermarket chains, who wanted next-day delivery on all orders, quite difficult when you have to decide four days in advance how many sausages you will need to supply on any given day.

Wherever there's a problem there's an opportunity. We asked Chris if he could commit the team to investigating how they could reduce the lead time to just one day, so that they could deliver on customer orders without having to anticipate demand in advance. He was adamant that this wasn't possible. The best the team could do was to try to reduce manufacturing lead times from four days to three, something unheard of in the industry at that time, and he said that anything less would be utterly impossible. This didn't seem much like a breakthrough to us and we needed to find a way to get Chris and his team to see this as "a story" rather than "the truth."

Later that morning, one of Chris's team, Alf, joined us for a tour of the plant. As we went round the impressive but cramped premises, Alf happened to mention that he had been a high-street butcher until the previous year. He'd had to close the small family business his father had started, ironically because of increased competition from the major supermarket chains that he now helped to supply. Out of curiosity, we asked if Alf had made sausages in his shop. He replied that he had and that he'd prided himself on his high-quality sausages, which he'd been able to make in well under an hour.

Back in Chris's office, we wrote up on a whiteboard two columns, one headed "possible" and the other "impossible." Under the word impossible we wrote "one-day lead time" and under possible, "three-day lead time." We then asked Chris, "If three days is possible and one day is impossible, what do we make of Alf's one-hour sausages?"

He was stunned. Several half-formed "ah buts" didn't quite make it out of his mouth. After a few moments, he was able to speak. "Let's see if we can figure out what a manufacturing process that delivered sausages in under a day would look like," he said. He had got the message and this completely transformed his view of what was possible.

The team joined us for the afternoon and by the end of the day were convinced that, even though it would require a complete overhaul of the plant, manufacturing sausages in under one day from raw material to delivery was not only possible, but would present many other benefits. The main direct benefit would be the ability to manufacture to order for next-day delivery without having to anticipate customer demands four days in advance. If implemented, their ideas would also free up a great deal of space on the site that was currently used for storing in-process sausagemeat and the associated refrigeration plant. Furthermore, it would save a large amount of energy and money currently spent on keeping all that meat cool for three days longer than necessary. In addition, those extra three days would be added to the shelf life, something customers were always looking for. The do-how map for Chris and the team is in Figure 10.

Chris had been stuck (in fact he was in denial about being stuck; it was his director who realized that he was stuck) because he couldn't visualize a breakthrough. He liked to work in a particular way and feared new approaches. Simply hearing from Alf that sausages could be made in under an hour (something he already knew if he allowed himself to) shattered his fixed mindset and meant that he and his team could set about creating a positive vision for what the team could do. They had identified what they needed to do to make a major breakthrough simply by holding out the possibility that such a breakthrough was possible and exploring what this opened up. The changes needed to implement their plans were too radical for the current management and the company was taken over shortly afterward, so they did never did fully implement the plans they created that day. Even so, the group they are part of is now recognized as the most efficient manufacturer of sausages in the United Kingdom.

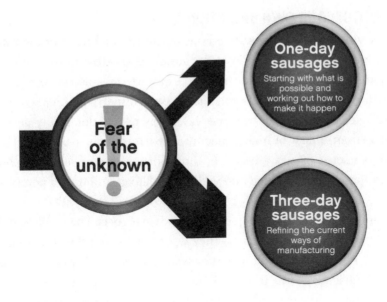

Figure 10   Chris's do-how map

TRY THIS: WHAT DO YOU REALLY WANT?

If anything were possible, what would you want to make possible?

Write down all your answers to this question. Don't edit yourself, just get everything down on paper. Try to write down at least 20 things or fill a couple of sheets of paper.

When you look at what you have written, how does it change the breakthrough you want to make? Are you thinking out of possibility or out of impossibility?

SPELL OUT YOUR OWN BREAKTHROUGH

A few years ago, we encountered one of the regional heats of the world arm-wrestling championship. What struck us was that most of the participants had one hugely developed arm with enormous muscles, but the other arm was no different than a typical man's and looked withered by comparison. In the same way, many people don't fully develop that extraordinary human capacity called intention. No matter how keen our sense of awareness or how quickly we get into action, without intention we are lop-sided and will fail to deliver on our full potential.

In our experience, most people don't have clear goals. They will describe their problems and the actions they want to take, but they don't necessarily have a clear view of how they want things to be. This is what sets apart true leaders. Just think of James Dyson or Steve Jobs – they knew exactly what they wanted and what they wanted changed the world.

Taking the time to spell out your breakthrough can make the difference between success and failure. You can do this on your own, by picturing your breakthrough goals and then challenging yourself to make them positive, precise possibilities. However, it's often easier to clarify the breakthrough in conversation with someone who will challenge your thinking and particularly your assumptions. When you spell out your breakthrough, you give yourself the opportunity to make the choices you want by bringing to life the alternative path, the upper fork of the do-how map. If your breakthrough isn't clear, you are always in danger of being hijacked by unconscious goals and limited by your hidden rules.

> **Taking the time to spell out your breakthrough can make the difference between success and failure**

TRY THIS: SPELL OUT YOUR BREAKTHROUGH

Take a look at the breakthrough goal that you wrote down earlier. Examine it using the four Ps to make sure that you have a picture of the positive, precise possibility for the breakthrough you want to make.

Create a mental **picture** – if you can imagine, it you can probably achieve it. Creating a mental picture allows you to fill in the blanks. If you can, find a role model who embodies the behavior you want to exhibit. Questions to ask include:

- What will things look like when I've made the breakthrough?

- How will I feel?

- How do I need to behave and think to achieve my breakthrough?

State the **positive** goal – state your breakthrough in terms of what you want rather than what you don't want. A positive goal creates a positive mental picture and makes it easier to achieve the goal. Identify any negative self-talk that is getting in your way and find the antidote that can encourage you to behave in a way that is consistent with the breakthrough you want to make. Questions to ask include:

- If I don't want... (e.g., criticism), what do I want? (e.g., positive feedback)

- If I had less... what would I have more of?

Clarify the **precise** details – challenge any vague descriptions. Hidden rules lurk in the gaps left by vague language. Precise details allow to you monitor your progress more easily. Questions to ask include:

- When precisely, what precisely, who precisely, where precisely?

- What do I mean by...? E.g., better communication – better in what way? Communication about what, between whom?

Identify what you want to make **possible** – make sure that your breakthrough is a statement of the difference you want to make rather than the actions you will take. Don't allow yourself to be trapped in problem thinking. Questions to ask include:

- If anything were possible, what would I want?

- What will my actions make possible that isn't possible now?

- What difference do I want to make?

Chapter 6

THE FISH SEE THE
WATER AT LAST

How to uncover your
hidden rules

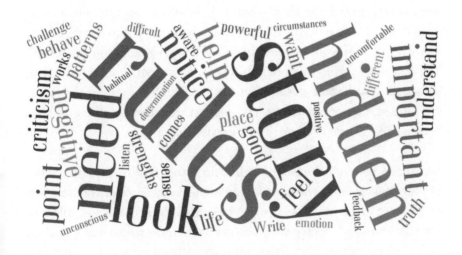

Uncover your hidden rules

There is a story about a fish and frog who meet in a pond. The fish asks the frog what he has seen in his travels beyond the pond. The frog tells him all about the grass and the birds and the sun, all things the fish is unfamiliar with. The fish is fascinated, and asks, "Is there is anything we have here that the creatures beyond the pond do not have?" The frog replies, "Beyond the pond there is very little water other than that which falls from the sky, whereas we are surrounded by water." The fish looks puzzled. "Water? What's water?" he asks.

It's not surprising that the fish should wonder what water is when he's been surrounded by it all his life. It has become so familiar that he doesn't even notice it and is surprised when it is pointed out to him. However, contain your laughter in case you end up laughing at yourself. The fish is no different from you or me. To a greater or lesser extent, we are all in the same predicament as the fish. We swim in the sea of our hidden rules and what we have been surrounded by all our life has become, like the nose on our face, invisible to us.

You can see your rules but, like the fuzzy tip of your nose that is in the center of your field of vision, you have simply stopped noticing them because you see them so frequently. They are the internal dialogue that is so familiar to you that you stop noticing that they are there in the background, guiding your choices and decisions. Your rules are difficult for you to notice, not because they are tough to spot, but because they are so obvious.

Your rules have been there in the background (or even, like your nose, the foreground) all the time, gently shepherding you, but the fact of their presence never quite makes it into your conscious mind. Your hidden rules are thoughts that are so well known you have stopped hearing them. They take on the status of truth or laws of the universe. But they are thoughts, not truths. And when you are brave enough to challenge them, you can break free of their limitations.

Hidden rules are both invisible and blindingly obvious. To uncover them we need to understand a little more about how they manage this amazing feat of being two totally opposite things at the same time. The secret lies in the stories we tell ourselves.

Your hidden rules are thoughts that are so familiar you have stopped noticing them

THE POWER OF STORIES

In April 1968, shortly after the assassination of Martin Luther King, schoolteacher Jane Elliott decided to help her pupils understand how it felt to be discriminated against. The children in her class were all white and from an area with few black people, so they had not experienced the kind of discrimination toward black people common in some other parts of the United States at the time. She explained that they were going to do an exercise and divided her class into two groups, those with blue eyes and those with brown eyes. She told them that for the purpose of the exercise the children with blue eyes would be treated as superior and given special privileges. They were encouraged only to play with children with the same eye color and to ignore those with brown eyes. Elliot made a point of praising children with blue eyes during the day and singling out anyone with brown eyes for chastisement. She also gave some pseudo-scientific, but purely bogus, explanations as to why people with blue eyes are more intelligent. All the exercise was meant to simulate was what it was like to be discriminated against.

What was surprising was that the children did not only play along with the exercise. Elliott noticed how their characters and even their academic performance changed according to the group they had been assigned to. Children who were normally quiet and reserved but who had been allocated to the superior group became more vocal and bossy. Intelligent children who just happened to have brown eyes struggled with tasks that they would normally complete with ease. She switched the roles the next day and told the children that in fact it was children with brown eyes who were superior. Despite the obvious pretense, she observed the exact same result, although this time it was the blue-eyed children who seemed less sure of their abilities and the brown-eyed ones who became more outgoing and assertive.

The exercise caused some controversy, but has been repeated numerous times in a wide range of settings to help people understand the dangers of discrimination. The results have been the same, with many intelligent and well-educated people reporting that they felt it difficult to resist the power of the stereotyping.

Stories are powerful and there are none more powerful than those we tell ourselves. What happened in Jane Elliott's class illustrates the power of stories to create the rules we play by. If we are told that we are inferior, we create rules for our behavior that are consistent with being inferior. If we are told that people with blue eyes are more intelligent, we start to believe it and behave according to rules that reinforce that story. Only when we are aware of the stories we tell ourselves can we see how our hidden rules flow from them and why they are so well hidden from us that we haven't noticed them before.

YOUR STORY MAKES SENSE

Take a look at this picture. What do you see?

Perhaps you see two hearts, or Homer Simpson kissing himself in a mirror, or even a Buddhist *stupa*. These are all replies that people have given when we have shown them this image. Whatever you do see, you are bringing that meaning to the picture, which is simply a random inkblot. The same is true of anything we experience. We bring meaning that isn't actually there. Have you ever leaned back on a summer's day and picked out faces or the shapes of animals in the clouds? Or perhaps you have looked up at night and traced the constellations of stars? You know full well that there are no faces in the clouds and that the choice of which stars belong to which constellations is merely arbitrary, but the human mind has an intense desire and capacity to make sense out of the world around us. We need a story. That is why when we are shown random inkblots we can construct some kind of meaning where there is none. Whatever you see, it says more about what is going on in your mind than about the image on the page.

Psychologists have come a long way in understanding how the mind works. Where they once looked to categorize us into different types, such as introverted or extroverted, they have more recently started to uncover how the stories we tell ourselves influence the way we see the world and the way we behave. Whether we are aware of it or not, each of us has our own story of how the world works, a kind of narrative of what is true. We are usually completely unaware that our story is a only a story because it becomes our truth and so seems obvious to us.

Your story is a mental map of how things are and a model for reality as you perceive it. Quite understandably, you behave in a way that makes sense given how you see the world. Some of your story will be based on verifiable facts that would still make sense when compared with other people's stories. For example, part of your story might be that the sun rises in the morning and sets in the evening. While most people will agree with that, it remains a story. It is not true in any absolute sense; it is simply an explanation that makes sense to you, from your perspective. If you spoke to someone who lived north of the Arctic Circle where for part of the year the sun doesn't set each day, it wouldn't match their experience of reality. They would need a different story to make sense of their world. And their story also isn't true, it's only another explanation that makes sense of their world. A scientist might explain that the sun neither rises nor sets, rather the earth rotates on its axis, obscuring the sun for part of the day.

There are other parts of your story that wouldn't make sense to other people. Your story might be that it's impossible to change. There are other people who would disagree with this and point to the changes they have made and they have seen others make.

Where these stories come from and whether they are an accurate reflection of the world around us isn't really the point, though. The point is that each of us carries around with us a mental model of how the world works and that we will always behave in a way that is consistent with that model. That is where our hidden rules come from. We make sense of the world through our story and we play the game of life by hidden rules that fit with our story of how the world works.

For example, suppose someone has a story that the results they achieve can be improved through perseverance and small, incremental changes. They will tend to be less disheartened by setbacks, which they interpret as an indication of their need to identify incremental improvements. By working hard at this they improve the probability of success and so reinforce their own story. Any setback will be seen as an invitation to persevere and they will appear to outsiders as having a rule to learn from failure and never back down, even when things get tough.

On the other hand, suppose someone else has an internal story that success comes only from talent and inspiration and that no amount of hard work can make up for the lack of talent. They will tend to interpret a failure as a confirmation that they don't have the talent needed to be a success. It is then quite rational that they should give up or become defensive when things don't go well. Giving up when the going gets tough starts to look like a rule, something they must or should do because it makes sense given what they believe to be true.

What is particularly interesting is how, by changing a story only slightly, we can change the way we behave and get different results. In one study in the United States, people who were underperforming and lacked belief in their ability to make changes were shown evidence that success comes through determination and incremental improvements rather than raw talent. Remarkably, their performance improved dramatically compared to other, similar people who received intensive support and training. The reason is that the intensive support and training simply reinforced the story those people already had, one that told them that they didn't have the talent required. It was the story that needed to change. Those who were told that success comes from dedication in applying incremental changes believed that it was true, which meant that they actually did follow through on any small setbacks to make the changes needed to turn failure into success. They didn't quit because from the perspective of the new story, quitting didn't make sense.

YOUR STORY, YOUR RULES

Many people find that their story manifests itself as a kind of inner voice or self-talk. Your story can be like your best friend who whispers good advice in your ear when you need it, or like your worst enemy whose criticism and words of doubt constantly undermine you. The psychological concepts of the inner critic or the inner child both point to the underlying stories we tell ourselves. Other people's stories come more in the form of images or movies that get played over and over in their mind. The one thing that is certain is that when you notice your story it will be very familiar. It will be something you have been saying or imagining for many years. You have been practicing and fine-tuning this story your whole life and for this reason you will also be very attached to it.

> Your story can be like your best friend who whispers good advice in your ear when you need it, or like your worst enemy whose criticism and words of doubt constantly undermine you

Each person's story is unique but, just like in novels or movies, there are some common themes or genres. Some stories are positive and life affirming and others are negative and limiting. Most people's stories are a mixture of the two. If we can spot the patterns in our own thinking, we are halfway to understanding what is really driving our actions and to being able to step outside the rules so that we can make the changes we want.

Just listen to people and you will hear their stories. Some of the most common stories we have heard many times are:

I'm superior to other people

I'm inferior to other people

I'm the same as other people

I'm different from everyone else

People like me

People don't like me

Whatever I do I will succeed

Whatever I do I will fail

People are going to find out that I'm useless

People value me for who I am

People only value me for my contribution

Hard work pays off in the end

Only talented people succeed and I'm not talented

The world is a safe place and people are friendly

The world is a dangerous place and people are unfriendly

Everything turns out well in the end

Things always go wrong

I'm the way I am because of my parents

I'm the way I am because of my job

I'm lucky – good things happen to me

I'm unlucky – bad things happen to me

Change is easy

Change is impossible

I matter more than other people.

I need things to be a particular way to be happy

There is one story that is so pervasive and debilitating that we will devote the whole of the next chapter to understanding and challenging it:

There is nothing I can do – I am the powerless victim of circumstances and other people's behavior

Of course, people's individual stories are much richer and have lots of personal details and context. What is important to recognize is that our background narrative is our way of making sense of the world and our place in it. The story is neither entirely true nor entirely untrue. It's simply a lens through which we view the world. It determines what we think of as important, what we pay attention to, and how we respond to the world. It defines the rules by which we play our life. We behave in a way that is consistent with the story we tell ourselves about the world.

Remember that there are three types of rules that flow from any story and guide or limit the way we can respond to any situation:

➠ **Unconscious intention** – our story tells us what it is important to achieve and what it is important to avoid. This defines our unconscious intention or goals and limits what we think is desirable or even possible.

119

➠ **Limited awareness** – our story tells us what to pay attention to and is the lens through which we interpret what we perceive. This limits what we notice and helps us filter out what isn't important.

➠ **Habitual action** – we behave in a way that is consistent with our story in order to achieve what our story tells us is important. This limits the range of actions or behaviors that we are likely to choose regardless of the circumstances.

THE SUBTLE TRAP

Your hidden rules are thoughts, not truths. What is surprising is that the very ways of thinking and behaving that your rules drive you toward will tend to reinforce whatever story you have that has led to your rules in the first place. This results in an internal consistency that makes it seem as though your rules really are the truth. This is what makes them so difficult to spot and is why they don't crumble easily when challenged.

Your hidden rules are thoughts, not truths

Because your rules tell you what it is important to notice, you filter out information that doesn't appear to be important. In other words, because you look for certain things you are more likely to see them, and you won't notice or give weight to evidence that doesn't fit in with your current view. Therefore your rules determine your awareness of reality. You see the world not as it is, but filtered through your story of how it is. Your rules also tell you what is possible and impossible, what is desirable and undesirable. If you cannot even imagine that some goal is attainable, it is unlikely that you will try to achieve it. If you believe that it is not possible for a machine to fly, then why would you try to build an aeroplane? If you believe that it is inconceivable to change something about your work, why would you try to alter it?

John has the idea that people in general are unfriendly. He has the expectation that when he meets people for the first time, they will not necessarily like him and so he is on his guard. Remember, we're not saying that this is necessarily a conscious thought; it's most likely an unconscious belief, a kind of whisper in the ear that guides his behavior. If he has not turned to see this hidden thought, he will not see people's behavior toward him as it is, but will interpret everything through this distorted lens. Consequently, he will behave in a way that confirms his original thought.

John's ideas about other people mean that he comes across as cool and defensive toward those he meets. He doesn't engage in conversation easily, nor does he show much interest in new people. This in turn discourages them from being open and friendly to him. Since he is on the lookout for signs of unfriendliness, he notices their negative reaction. When it is pointed out to him that the idea that people are unfriendly is only a thought, not the truth, he points to his own very real experience as evidence for the validity of his views.

You see the world not as it is, but filtered through your story of how it is

What John sees and hears is really a reflection of something in himself, but he takes it as confirmation of his view that people are unfriendly. This is the subtle trap that our stories and hidden rules lead us into. We will always find evidence that the way we see the world is correct. The tendency is that the first and most obvious place we ought to look in order to understand the difficulties we experience – our own ways of thinking – is usually the last place we consider. It is as if some brilliant magician were constantly turning our awareness in any direction but the one in which we will notice the rabbit that she is about to pull out of the hat.

HIDDEN RULES LOSE THEIR POWER WHEN YOU CAN SEE THEM

Once you spot your habitual patterns of thought and behavior, they lose their hold over you. This is not magic; it's simply that most of the power of your hidden rules comes from the fact that you are not aware of them. As you become aware of your rules as thoughts rather than truths, you take back your ability to choose your behavior and to respond to any situation in a way that is likely to get you the best result. This doesn't happen instantly. You've had a lifetime to tell yourself a particular story about the way the world works and to find the rules of success consistent with that story. You've put many hours into practicing to perfection ways of behaving that flow from those rules. However, as you gradually become more aware of any rule, you will see clearly that it is a thought that is only helpful in some cases, not a truth that is always true. Then you will naturally start to notice opportunities to choose behavior that serves you better.

Once you spot your habitual patterns of thought and behavior, they lose their hold over you

One time we were in the Czech Republic running a training program for a division of Ford that made car radiators. We had a free afternoon and decided to spend some time exploring the streets of Ostravia, in the east of the country. We came across a mime artist performing in one of the city squares. Part of his act was that he had an imaginary dog who would pull him around as he tried to go about various tasks. He had a stiffened dog lead that would suddenly pull off to one side and even jump up as the imaginary dog appeared to stand on its hind legs to greet its owner. He struggled to control the dog without the ability to anticipate where it would go next as it pulled this way and that. The mime was very convincing and after a while it was easy to forget that there wasn't in fact a real dog on the end of the lead. Our hidden rules are like this imaginary dog. They pull us all over the place and because we can't see them they have much more influence over us than they otherwise would. If the dog was real, there would be no joke, as the mime artist would be able to see its movements and react to them with ease.

Let's see how this works in practice. We are sure you have met people who are uptight and highly sensitive to any form of criticism. They may have the idea that they are "not good enough." Darrell is one such person. He was always immaculately dressed in a designer suit, highly polished shoes, and a precisely knotted tie that cost more than most people's weekly wages. His office was uncluttered and he had a neatly drawn list of priorities on his whiteboard, with the ones he had completed marked off in red. To anyone visiting him for the first time, he looked like a man on top of his brief as corporate director of a growing business services firm.

However, beneath the polished image things were starting to fall apart. He confided in us that he never quite considered himself up to the job and still felt like "a kid in short pants who would be found out any time." His mind was constantly on the lookout for criticism and he was dreading the approaching personal review with his boss. What was clear listening to him was that his biggest critic was his own internal voice telling him that he wasn't good enough and that he would be uncovered as a fraud sooner or later. We witnessed several occasions when what might have been taken as innocuous comments from another person he interpreted as potentially critical. His colleagues and his boss had started to see him as defensive, prickly, and closed to new ideas.

It is not difficult to spot what is happening here. Because Darrell's unconscious intention is to avoid criticism, he finds criticism unbearable. He does not have a clear goal for what "good enough" looks like, because his unconscious narrative is that he can never be good enough. He does not consider that he has achieved anything and so he feels vulnerable to criticism. He defends himself from criticism, which means that those colleagues who do want to criticize him tend to be quite forceful to make sure that their point gets through. So he confirms that he really does need to avoid criticism. In other words, his rules lead him to think and behave in ways that mean he is more likely to attract criticism and to notice it when it is given. His story leads to rules that drive behavior that confirms his story.

When Darrell had the courage to examine his thoughts, he found that they were just that, ideas about what might be helpful rather than unbreakable truths that were applicable at all times and in all places. We remember well the conversation where he finally tuned in to the almost continual inner voice of criticism that accompanied him throughout the day. This voice drove him to have high standards, but also undermined his confidence and built an almost impenetrable shield against all genuine external criticism. Nevertheless, when faced with the evidence and feedback from his colleagues, he couldn't deny that he was good at many aspects of his job. We helped him reframe criticism as a positive experience. When he decided to seek out feedback proactively, it still felt uncomfortable, but he was able to let go of that discomfort as he nurtured his curiosity about the areas in which his colleagues felt he could improve.

An unexamined rule drives habitual behavior, which leads to confirmation of our story. An examined rule leads to choice about the actions most likely to lead to a favorable result. In the same way as Darrell, we all have habitual patterns to our thinking and behavior that lead us to find evidence that our story is true and that our rules are both sensible and important. Our hidden rules are thoughts that seem like universal truths. However, when we become aware of our patterns of thinking, when we really acknowledge our rules as thoughts rather than truths, they lose their power over us. This doesn't mean that they go away, but that when we understand them we have a choice. The clearer we are about the stories we tell ourselves and the hidden rules that guide how we behave, the easier it is to let go of them when we want to make a breakthrough.

Fortunately, there are many ways to deepen the understanding you have of the inner narrative that drives your choices and to uncover your hidden rules. The challenge is to learn to listen. When you do spot your rules as rules, they will hit you between the eyes like nothing you have experienced before. Some of the most powerful approaches that we have found to work well are described in the rest of this chapter.

TRY THIS: SPOT YOUR HIDDEN RULES

Take a moment now to write down what you think your hidden rules are. It can help to ask someone who knows you well to give you some feedback to see if you are in the right area.

> **Intention** – what is it important for you to achieve and what is it important for you to avoid?
>
> **Awareness** – what do you pay attention to and how do you interpret what you perceive?
>
> **Action** – what do you habitually do in order to achieve what is important to you?

IDENTIFY WHAT YOU ARE AVOIDING

While most hidden rules are helpful in at least some circumstances, rules that cause us to avoid or move away from certain goals are major road blocks to success. These negative rules lead us to set negative goals and spotting them is an important step to releasing our potential and developing our do-how.

Negative thoughts will be at the root of most of your background anxieties and concerns in life, the places where you get most stuck and the things you most struggle with. You might be certain that you have clear, positive goals that you are excited about and that are spelt out in enough detail for you to visualize them. But we all have a few negative thoughts lurking somewhere in our unconscious. Like all aspects of our story, these ideas are there to help us and protect us, but they somehow get things the wrong way around. By spotting and challenging negative aspects of your story, you can overcome some of the major obstacles to your own growth and development.

Some of the most common negative thoughts we come across include:

I mustn't upset anyone

I mustn't be weak

I mustn't lose out to other people

125

I must avoid mistakes

I must avoid criticism

I mustn't ask for what I want

I mustn't fail

I must avoid not knowing the answer

I mustn't be rejected

I must avoid needing anyone/anything

I mustn't be wrong

I must avoid losing

I must avoid risks

I need/must have...

Of course, nobody likes feeling this way. Each of these thoughts is accompanied by fear and anxiety and we can't perform well if we are dogged by them. They might motivate us in the way that a snarling dog can motivate us to run, but they are a poor substitute for a positive and energizing story of what is important.

These kinds of thoughts crop up in organizations where there is what might be called a "blame culture." The habitual thought that runs through the culture is something like "I mustn't get anything wrong." This debilitates people, stifles creativity, and makes it difficult to have honest conversations about what needs to change or improve.

The last thought on the list is slightly different from the others. Sometimes a negative hidden rule comes up as a need. If you persistently feel that you are lacking something and that troubles you, then it is possible that you are in the grip of a negative rule. We are not talking about transitory needs here. If you are driving a long way and think "I need some fuel," you may well do so. We mean those needs that are like bottomless pits and can never be satisfied, regardless of whether they are objectively being filled or not. We are sure that you have met people who seem to require constant praise or who need to be told again and again that they are valued. Like hungry ghosts, they feel that they lack something and no matter how much you or anyone else gives them, they are never satisfied. Behind that need is no doubt some story such as "I'm a failure" or "Nobody likes me."

The question to ask yourself is: "Am I moving toward what is important to me because it excites me, or am I moving away from something that I fear or a feeling of lack?" Spotting these patterns won't immediately change things. Old habits die hard, but once you spot them you will have a different perspective and more choice about how you respond to situations that trigger your hidden rules. Over time, you will start to comprehend each rule as a thought rather than a truth.

TRY THIS: SPOTTING NEGATIVE THOUGHTS

This exercise will help you start the process of spotting any negative elements of your story. It does require honesty. It is easy to find ways of putting a positive spin on any of your answers.

Ask yourself: "What is important to me?" Think about times when you felt excited or spurred into action. Write a list of at least ten things that are important to you.

Now, look at each item on the list and ask yourself: "Why is this important to me?" Write down at least three short answers to this question for each item. Write down the first thing that comes into your mind.

You will end up with around 30 short statements of what is important to you and why it is important.

For each of these statements, ask yourself: "Is this something I feel positive about and am moving toward, or is it something I feel negative about and I want to avoid or move away from?" Does getting what you want feel exciting or is it that the fear of losing it fills you with dread? Mark each answer as positive, negative, or not sure.

Look over your answers and see whether there is a pattern of one or two things you are trying to avoid. Write these down. The chances are that you are starting to close in on one or two negative parts of your story that are holding you back.

Do the insights from this exercise change the hidden rules that you wrote down at the end of the previous chapter?

Look back at the hidden rules you wrote down earlier. Does this exercise change your view?

LOOK IN THE PLACES THAT MAKE YOU UNCOMFORTABLE

Whatever irritates us or scares us tells us about ourselves. Your negative emotions are an accurate and reliable record of your hidden rules, and if you take the time to explore what you find uncomfortable, you will start to see the patterns of thought that lie underneath them. Moments when you finally notice your emotions and recognize them for what they are – the ultimate in feedback, the final word in insider knowledge – are so precious because they make the invisible visible. They point directly and instantly to the source of what limits you. They reveal your ignorance of what really drives you and in doing so they open up the choice to step beyond those limitations. Not only that, but you'll be shocked by how stupendously obvious what you've been looking for is. Your unconscious motivations are not at all hidden from you, it's just that they are so completely obvious that you don't notice what an incredible hold they have over your patterns of thought and behavior.

What irritates or scares us tells us about ourselves

We were working with a team at a large manufacturer of construction machinery. During a meeting two members of the team, Sam and Steve, received some feedback on a project they had been involved with. They had stepped in to help with the project, which was getting into difficulties. One of the directors they reported to said, "You've done a great job, but some staff felt you were a little heavy handed and they would have liked to have been involved more in the decisions that were taken."

Sam reacted positively to the feedback. She mainly heard "You've done a great job." That's what mattered to her, and she listened with some pride to the advice from the director on how to do even better next time.

However, Steve didn't even hear "great job," all he heard was "heavy handed." "How dare they!" he grumbled afterward. "If it weren't for me they'd be in big trouble." He was filled with anger and could barely contain his emotions as he pretended to listen to the director's advice. Same words, completely different reactions.

If you want to know where to place your attention in order to really understand yourself, simply look at what you react to. That's the blind spot. That's where you've really got your energy invested.

Each time you notice discomfort – are bothered by a situation or sensation – a little bit of what really drives you is being revealed. That is why exercises such as the next one are so powerful. If you are honest with yourself (and not everyone is), they force you to look in places that are uncomfortable and unfamiliar. In fact, if the exercise isn't uncomfortable, you probably haven't been entirely honest with yourself – now does that make you uncomfortable?

TRY THIS: WHAT MAKES YOU UNCOMFORTABLE?

Think of three occasions when you experienced a negative or uncomfortable emotion - anger, frustration, sadness, fear, apathy - and you didn't like the result. Write down your answers to the following:

- What emotion did you experience?

- What thoughts did you have?

- How did you behave?

Take a look at what you have written. Is there a pattern to your feelings, thoughts, and behavior?

If you have trouble recognizing the thoughts, ask yourself, "What must someone who feels like that and behaves like that be thinking?" Try talking this over with a friend and see if you can spot something that seems familiar and obvious to you but is limiting your behavior. Your rules are easier to spot for people who don't share them, so talking about your thoughts with someone you trust to challenge you can be very helpful and illuminating.

For the same reason, listening to feedback from others can be beneficial. Think of times when you have received feedback that may have wounded you or shocked you. Any time you have a strong emotional reaction there is the possibility that your hidden rules are being challenged, so that is a good place to look.

Write down any insights you have from this exercise. Does this change your view of the hidden rules that you wrote down earlier?

LOOK AT THE FLIP SIDE OF YOUR STRENGTHS

Your hidden rules are the source of your success, but they are also the ways in which you limit yourself. The greater the strength and the less aware we are of exercising that strength habitually, the more likely we are to be limited by it. The danger is that our strengths can push us further into the mire rather than getting us out of it. If you understand your strengths and how those strengths become limitations, you can start to narrow down where to look for your hidden rules.

The next exercise will help you identify how your strengths and limitations interrelate.

TRY THIS: STRENGTHS AND LIMITATIONS

Take a piece of paper and on one side write down three of your strengths. No doubt you are quite proud of your strengths. After all, they are what have got you to where you are today. For example, you might feel that you are careful, meticulous, and have an eye for detail. Or you might describe yourself as decisive, courageous, and determined. Whatever comes to mind, write it down.

Now turn the piece of paper over and reflect on how each of those strengths can become a limitation in some circumstances. If you are "careful," that is clearly a strength, but can you imagine circumstances in which it pays to throw caution to the wind? Or what about decisiveness? Are there times when decisiveness gets in the way? The part to watch for is the "always, in all circumstances," the musts and mustn'ts, shoulds and shouldn'ts. That's what turns a thought into a rule and that's what will limit you.

Look back at the hidden rules you wrote down earlier. Does this exercise change your view?

A few people struggle with this exercise. If you can't think of any strengths or find this exercise difficult, simply recognize the uncomfortable emotion you are experiencing. See if you can spot the thought behind the emotion. It's most probably a negative part of your story, such as "I'm useless at everything," pointing to a hidden rule such as "It's wrong to boast."

THE ROOTS OF OUR DISCOMFORT

We all share certain experiences that shape our hidden rules as we develop from birth through childhood to become an adult. It can be useful to understand these shared experiences so that you know what to look for. Just to be clear, we aren't suggesting that you examine your own development as a child. We don't think that's necessary or even helpful for the purpose of understanding what you are experiencing as a mature, well-functioning adult. There is a whole body of knowledge on childhood development and the formation of personality, but we don't need to go into all that to see that, whatever the specifics of your own history, there are some patterns everyone has in common and these can give us a starting point for looking at the broad roots of the negative emotions we experience.

We share an experience of being totally dependent on others for our basic needs as a baby. As we grow, we share the experience of becoming an independent human with the need to be loved and to feel good about who we are. Once we start to become independent as a teenager, we experience the need to take control of our life and break free from our parents. Because of these experiences, many rules form around our common human needs:

The need to feel safe and secure

The need for respect and self-esteem

The need for self-determination and personal control

Our desire to satisfy these basic needs is instinctive, and all of our stories and rules are intended to maximize them or protect us from losing them.

SAFETY AND SECURITY

In the early stages of childhood we are helpless, relying totally on our parents or other carers for nourishment, care, and shelter. We are dependent on others for every aspect of our wellbeing. Quite instinctively we understand this, if understand is the right word, and become distressed if these needs are not met. With our infant mind we are ill equipped to deal with the stress of those inevitable occasions when these needs aren't met, so we start to form patterns of thinking and behavior to avoid them. The extent to which these patterns develop will depend on the nature of the individual infant and the nurture that he or she receives. We met one man who, despite being very wealthy, always spoke as if he were down to his last penny. He never missed an opportunity to save money and drove an old, rusty car when he could have owned a Rolls-Royce. It seems pretty clear that his story was driven by a perceived lack of security.

RESPECT AND SELF-ESTEEM

A little later in life, we are still dependent on others for most or all of our needs, but we have a developing image of ourselves as individuals. We realize that we can cause reactions in others, good and bad. A certain amount of attention and acceptance from those around us is essential for us to thrive. And so, quite naturally, we start to create ways of thinking and behaving that boost our self-esteem and invite the love and respect of others. Any parent who has heard those inviting words "Look at me!" from a 6 or 7 year old will recognize the importance of love and self-esteem to the developing child. Part of many people's story will be around their self-esteem and some of their rules will be about how to look good in front of other people.

SELF-DETERMINATION AND CONTROL

Still later, as we approach adulthood, our sense of individuality grows to the point where we want to branch out, to become our own independent person. This again is a natural instinct. The desire here is to take control of our life. No longer do we want to live under the shadow of our parents' view of what makes sense of life, or be dependent on others for our wellbeing. We develop patterns of thinking and behavior that underpin our need to take control of our lives.

The balance of how our personality incorporates these three basic human experiences depends on a whole multitude of factors. These include our innate nature or genetic disposition, the nurture we receive during our childhood, the cultural milieu in which we are raised, and any traumatic or dramatic events we experience during our formative years. If you scratch the surface of any individual's behavior to look at the story behind it, you will most likely find one of these basic needs underlying it.

Identifying which of these three fundamental human needs is most at play in your life can help you to look in the right place to uncover your hidden rules. Whenever you experience any discomfort, you will find that one of these basic needs is being denied or is in danger of being lost. What is important is to get at the emotional reaction and the actual thoughts or self-talk that lie behind it, not your intellectual rationalization of why you feel that way.

However lucky we are, whatever is provided by our good fortune will never be enough to satisfy our unconscious needs. Someone who is driven by a need to be loved will never be loved enough. Someone who is really trying to prove to her mother that she is good enough will never feel happy so long as she fails to recognize what is really driving her behavior. While they remain hidden, our stories make us like bottomless buckets. We can never be filled, and the only way to feel satisfied is to recognize the story for what it is, and learn to let go.

PERSONALITY MODELS

There are a wide range of tools and personality profiling systems on the market, which can give insights into your habitual or preferred patterns of behavior and the thoughts that lie behind them. These include the Myers-Briggs type indicator, Belbin team profiles, Strengths Finder, and many other commercial tools. You may have completed one of these at some time in your career. Any of them can help, but the one that we prefer to use is the Enneagram (which simply means nine-pointed diagram), probably because it describes nine personality types in terms of the different kinds of narratives that people hold and because of the map that shows how the different personality types relate to each other. Our version of the Enneagram is given in Figure 11. It can be a useful starting point to see whether any of these types seems familiar. You can think of the nine personality types as genres. If you were watching a movie and it was described as a comedy, that would tell you something about the movie but not any of the detail. In the same way, while the general type may be applicable to you, your hidden rules will be unique.

There are many excellent books about the Enneagram and we would encourage you to take a closer look at some of these to broaden your understanding and identify how models such as this can help you.

Figure 11   Enneagram: nine different stories

	INTENTION	AWARENESS	ACTION
1	To be right/perfect	What is right/wrong?	Do the right thing
2	To be loved/liked	What do people need?	Help and support people
3	To be respected/admired	How do people see me?	Work hard to impress people
4	To be unique/special	How do I feel?	Imagine and create the new and special
5	To understand/know	Does this make sense?	Gather information and knowledge
6	To be safe/secure	What could go wrong?	Question everything and everyone ... ah but
7	To have fun/satisfaction	What are my options?	Do what is new and interesting
8	To be powerful/in control	What needs doing?	Take decisive action
9	To be in harmony/union	How do other people think and feel?	Blend into the background and avoid conflict

Figure 12 Hidden rules for the nine enneagram personality types

TRY THIS: THE ENNEAGRAM

Take a look at the nine descriptions of enneagram personality types in Figure 12. Choose one that seems similar to your approach to life. If there are several that stand out to you, look for patterns in Figure 11 to see whether the ones you have chosen are connected. If you aren't sure, ask a friend who knows you well enough to make some honest suggestions.

Look back at the hidden rules you wrote down earlier. Does this exercise change your view?

LISTEN TO YOURSELF

Your hidden rules mostly manifest as inner dialogue or self-talk. If you can listen in to that dialogue and hear it objectively, you can get an insight into your hidden rules. Remember that your rules are hidden in plain sight. They aren't difficult to spot, just so obvious that you don't realize they are there. What you don't notice is that you are making choices, and in doing so you are placing limits on what you can achieve. Listening to yourself can be difficult, but it can be done.

The awareness practice or mindfulness exercises discussed in Chapter 4 are a very powerful way to develop the capacity for turning your attention inward. If you practice these, over time you will start to notice patterns in the thoughts that interrupt your practice. There is a good chance that there will be some big clues to your hidden rules in this inner chatter. This takes time, however, and there is another way of listening in on your inner dialogue that yields results more quickly.

NOTICE YOUR JUDGMENTS

One way of thinking about your hidden rules is as judgments. Your mind is making judgments all the time. It is difficult to get through a few minutes without doing so. By judgments we mean thoughts along the lines of:

"This is good"

"That is bad"

"He should do this"

"She shouldn't do that"

"I like this"

"I don't like that"

You can listen for your judgments as you go through the day, but the most powerful way to spot them is to write about them. You might like to take some time now to complete the exercise below. You can do the exercise on your own, but it is even more powerful to debrief it with a friend who can challenge what you come up with.

TRY THIS: LOOK AT YOUR JUDGMENTS

Take one of the areas that you wrote down in the first exercise in this book, something where you want to make a breakthrough or you feel stuck. It doesn't matter what the subject is as long as it's something that matters to you and where you want to make a breakthrough.

Find a quiet place where you won't be disturbed and write for 15 minutes everything you believe about the situation, what has happened, what that means to you, what you want, what is possible, and what you can and can't do. Imagine you are talking to a really close friend and let whatever comes into your mind find its way onto paper.

Don't think too much and keep your pen moving even if you are writing nonsense. This helps to bypass your natural tendency to edit your thoughts. After 15 minutes, most people have filled at least two or three sheets of A4 paper.

When you have finished, take a break for at last a couple of hours and preferably for a couple of days, then go back to what you have written.

Look in your writing for any judgments, which are likely to point to your hidden rules. The words "should," "shouldn't," "must," "mustn't," and "can't" are dead giveaways, along with any absolute statements such as "always," "never," "everyone," "I had to...," or "It's not possible to..." Sometimes the language is more subtle and this is where it helps to have a close friend who can challenge you. The aim is to spot any statement where you seem to be mistaking a thought or a judgment for an absolute truth.

Summarize these statements and challenge them by asking: Is this really true? Are there occasions when it isn't true? Is there any truth in the opposite of what I am saying?

Examine any adjectives or adverbs. You have many alternatives to choose from when making descriptions. The specific words you use can tell you a great deal about your judgments. One person's "pushy" is another's "decisive." If you find yourself describing someone as "slow," could they also be called "meticulous" or "laid back?" We remember one client who always insisted on describing any instructions as "destructions." This told us much about his attitude to organizational procedures and pointed to a hidden rule that he had to always challenge authority.

Are there any judgments about yourself? The things that you repeatedly tell yourself are potentially vital clues to your hidden rules. See if you can spot a pattern to them. What do they tell you about your story and your rules?

It can be useful to repeat this exercise several times over a number of days and add any new thoughts.

Look back at the hidden rules you wrote down earlier. Does this exercise change your view?

SOFT SKILLS ARE HARD SKILLS

Sometimes people react against this recommendation to turn inward to examine their own deep-seated thoughts and motivations. The most common criticism is that it is self-indulgent, or that it might be seen as navel gazing. In our experience this is far from the case. Turning inward in this way requires a certain amount of courage and self-awareness and people do not always like what they find.

You've probably seen or heard of the program *This Is Your Life*. Well-known public figures met a series of people who had known them during their life. These people proceeded to relate interesting and often little-known facts about the celebrity's history. What they revealed was usually light-hearted, amusing, and sometimes quite flattering. The celebrity left with a large red book, their biography in the eyes of people who knew them.

Imagine that a similar book has been compiled about you, but rather than innocuous or celebratory highlights, this book contains what people really think of you, warts and all. You are being handed that book right now. How does it feel? Probably a good dose of excitement, but also a great big dollop of "Do I really want to read this?" thrown in for good measure. We actually do a version of this on some of our development workshops, and we can tell you that you can hear a pin drop as people receive their feedback from the other participants.

Who knows you better than yourself? No one. You already have an even more detailed and scarier version of that big red book, written by yourself, accounting for every experience, every emotion, every thought, and every action in your life – not only what people think of you, but what actually happened, what you actually thought, and most of all what you actually felt. And this is not just a book, but the technicolor, smellorama, full-works box set of DVDs as well! No wonder your head is like a barrel full of monkeys. You've got more archived material than the BBC stored up there.

So let's guess what happens when you turn inward. The action replays start. All sorts of things from your past run through your mind. And these aren't the boring, sedate, noneventful bits – you get the gory, excruciating bumps, crashes, and near-misses; painful experiences from the past that you'd rather forget; events that may have seemed innocuous at the time, but that from today's vantage point can seem awfully embarrassing.

TO GROW IS TO LET GO

Self-awareness can be painful, but it is also a blessing and a source of great strength. The point of all this is simply to see yourself as you are, but then to choose to let go when you need to. If you don't like what you find, then you have a chance to do something about it. Blissful ignorance – and there's really no such thing, otherwise you wouldn't be reading this book – isn't really an option if you want to grow. To grow is to let go and to let go you must know what you are holding on to.

> To grow is to let go and to let go you must know what you are holding on to

When you recognize this you can choose your behavior, rather than letting your behavior choose you. You can choose your own future or let that future choose you.

TRY THIS: LETTING GO

Take stock of what you have learned about yourself through the exercises in this chapter. You might want to revisit what you wrote about your hidden rules one more time.

You can't grow unless you let go. What are you willing to let go of in order to grow and make the breakthrough you want? Just to be clear, we're not talking about letting go of the qualities and behaviors that you see as your strengths. We're talking about letting go of having to exercise those qualities and behaviors regardless of whether they are helpful or not. This means letting go of the illusion that your hidden rules are absolute truths.

Chapter 7

YOUR POWER TO CHANGE
How to take responsibility
for the choices you make

Have you noticed how some people never complain whatever happens? They somehow seem to find the inner resources to see a way forward and carry on whatever difficulty or setback they face. They focus on what is positive, take whatever action is necessary to make the changes they want, and get people around them galvanized to deliver. On the other hand, there are other people who complain all the time. Whatever happens, it's somebody else's fault and there's nothing they can do about it. They hold on to their problems as cherished reasons why they don't ever have to change. Their perception is: "I have a problem, caused by someone or something out there that I can't do anything about." Does this apply to you sometimes?

Making change happen means being willing to step beyond knowing what to do and actually taking responsibility for doing something different. However, there are some habits of thought that are so universal and so damaging that they leave us feeling powerless to take any action. These are thoughts such as:

"There's nothing I can do"

"I'm the powerless victim of circumstances"

"It's someone else's behavior that is at fault"

"This problem can only be solved by someone else"

These thoughts destroy our sense that we have the power to change anything and leave us feeling hopeless and incapacitated.

Most people have thoughts like this sometimes. There are challenges that seem so overwhelming that even the most positive person might feel impotent. That's what it's like when we feel stuck and change seems impossible.

Nevertheless, the idea that there is nothing you can do is an illusion. It comes about because the thought "there is nothing I can do" becomes part of your story and therefore goes unchallenged. If you really believe that there is nothing you can do, then that thought leads you to focus on the things you *can't* do and confirms your original thought. But going along with the thought that you are powerless is a choice and it's not a choice you ever have to take. There are some things in life that you might have to accept, but being a powerless victim of circumstances or other people's behavior isn't one of them. There is always another option that you are free to take if you can spot these energy-sucking thoughts and see through them.

> **The choices you make in the here and now are your lever for influencing the future**

You have the power to change yourself and the power to change those things around you that you aren't satisfied with. Whether you consciously choose to exercise this power or not, the fabric of your life is woven from the consequence of every choice you have ever made. What you choose to do in the here and now is your lever for influencing the future. Taking responsibility for your choices is the very heart of developing do-how. Without this step, everything we have said so far is simply more know-how and, on its own, will change little.

WHAT ARE YOU GOING TO DO?

An old friend and colleague of Dave's, Tony Marmont, taught us everything we need to know about the power of personal responsibility. Whenever anyone started to complain about another person or a situation they didn't like, Tony would listen for a while, then ask, "So what are you going to do about it?" That usually stopped the conversation in its tracks, as the person realized that they were merely indulging in a bit of moaning and they really ought to get over whatever was bugging them or do something about it.

One thing that often happened when Tony challenged people this way was that they would say "But there is nothing I can do, it's the other guy who needs to change" or something similar. We need to remember how vague language hides all kinds of assumptions. What is missing from this statement is something like: "There's nothing I can do as long as I insist on everyone playing by my hidden rules and satisfying my emotional needs." That's usually much nearer the truth.

Dawn was stuck with a lack of resources to do her job properly, or at least that's the way she saw it. She is one of the most helpful and conscientious people we have ever met. Her hidden rule of always making everyone happy had seen her rise to be the head of a team responsible for the maintenance of a large property portfolio for a hospital trust. People liked Dawn because, whatever they wanted, she never said no.

A restructuring of the business had left her with 20 percent fewer staff and she was working 60 hours a week to ensure everything was running smoothly and, most importantly in her eyes, keep everyone happy. She was very unhappy herself and looked on the edge of a nervous breakdown when we met her. She felt powerless to do anything about her situation. When asked what she could do to change things, she couldn't see any way forward. In her mind, the only person who could sort the problem out was her boss. She reeled off a long list of attempts to persuade her boss to give her more resources so that she could do everything she wanted to do to keep everyone happy. She agreed that her boss wouldn't, and probably couldn't, give her the extra people she needed. We listened to her berate the senior management of the hospital, her colleagues, the government, and even the bankers, who in her eyes were responsible for the economic difficulties that led to her having fewer staff. Everyone else was to blame for the situation but her.

There may be some literal truth here in that the actions of these people had led to the circumstances that Dawn found herself in. But what we need to remember is that the results we get come from the interaction of reality with our own response. That's the part that Dawn had overlooked.

We asked Dawn if there was anything she could do that didn't involve asking her boss to give her more resources yet again. She sat in silence shaking her head, until one of her colleagues suggested that she could turn down some of the more outrageous requests people in the organization made of her team. He might as well have suggested that she buy some rocket-powered antigravity boots.

"I couldn't, it's just not in my character, that's the way I am," she said, the implication being that she had no choice in how she behaved. This was Dawn's myth and it's one that limits so many otherwise talented people. The idea that we have no choice, that we must behave like an automaton with no free will but to go along with our habitual response, is the most constraining thought of all. Dawn could do nothing to change the reality of the difficult economic climate, but she could do something about how she chose to react to that reality.

Dawn had simply never considered that it might be possible to say no or to deliver a little less than was being demanded. What was blindingly obvious to everyone else, at least as an option to be considered, was totally out of sight to her because it seemed so clear that there was nothing she could do. She had been trapped by the idea that the only person who could solve her problem was her boss. She had never genuinely asked herself the question: "What else can *I* do?"

During the discussion that followed, we found lots of examples of people saying no by prioritizing their work and delivering what was really important to the organization, rather than simply saying yes to everything. By understanding that some of the people who she respected most could say no in a very effective and positive way, Dawn started to see the possibility for herself. The feedback from colleagues opened up the idea of a breakthrough that she had never considered.

What is ironic is that one of the values of the organization was "delivering on priorities" and Dawn had been on a training program to teach her tools and techniques for prioritizing her work. She had simply not seen the relevance of this know-how to her own situation. She had been like one of those people who in the early days of steam railways had cried, "It's just not possible for human beings to travel that fast and survive!"

Over the next few weeks, Dawn took ownership of the situation and started to build a positive idea of how she could prioritize what the team worked on. This was a huge breakthrough for her. Everyone around her knew her as the person who could never say no. Dawn knew this too, and it was a huge revelation that it didn't have to be this way. For the first time in months, she felt that she had some power to change her situation.

WHERE'S THE PROBLEM?

What really gets in the way of us taking responsibility for making the choices that lead to a breakthrough is the idea that there really is "nothing I can do." What's hidden in this thought is the assumption that the only way things can change is if something else "out there" changes. It's the other guy, or the external circumstances, that need to change. We might have an idea of how we would like things to be different, but in terms of how other people will behave or a vague wish that somehow the situation was different – "My boss should give me more resources, the hospital trust should prioritize building maintenance, if the economy would pick up everything would be fine," and so on. This thought makes us a passive victim of circumstances and of other people's behavior. Unless people buy in to our idea that they need to change, nothing changes and we remain stuck.

When we decide to wait for circumstances to change, we might be waiting for a long time. If we really think that the solution to our problems lies "out there," we feel powerless to act and that's when we need a breakthrough. However, there is another way to look at things that changes everything.

Imagine for a moment that you are driving along the road on the way to a meeting, when a slow-moving car pulls out in front of you. You adjust your speed and trundle along at half the speed limit. You look for a place to overtake, but you are on a winding road with high hedges and you simply can't see far enough ahead to overtake safely. You can't understand why this person is going so slowly. You aren't likely to be late for your appointment, but you can't bear to go at this speed. You start to get frustrated. Does this sound familiar?

So how would you describe this problem? For most people it would be something like: "I'm frustrated because the person in front is driving too slowly." You blame the driver in front. You are a victim of his driving too slowly. Obviously, there is nothing you can do about this situation because the person in front is the cause of the problem. The problem is definitely the other guy and he needs to pull over or speed up!

But what about the person in front, how would he describe the problem? Equally obviously: "I am feeling annoyed because the person behind is driving too close." He would blame you, the person behind. The problem is definitely the idiot in the car behind who insists on driving too fast, too close, and needs to slow down. It's all so obvious. What could possibly be wrong with that?

Suppose another, even slower driver pulls out, and the original slow driver is now forced to slow down even further. Perhaps everyone is admiring the scenery, or the road is slightly wet and both the slow drivers are anxious about skidding on the bends. Whatever the reason, do you think the original slow driver will be frustrated by the driver going even more slowly in front? We think not. In fact, he may even feel slightly relieved of the pressure to go "too fast" coming from the maniac behind. So if you are frustrated by the slow driver in front of you and that slow driver isn't frustrated by the even slower driver ahead, where is the problem? Is the problem really that the car in front is going too slowly? Or is it that you like to be in control and get frustrated when you can't go at the speed you want. The real problem, if you're being honest, is: "I'm frustrated because I like to get my own way and at the moment I can't." That's somewhat of a turnaround from where we started a few minutes ago.

Figure 13 Where's the problem?

When you turn around and start looking for the answer to your problem where it can actually be found, in your own way of thinking and behaving, that's when the possibility of change opens up. When you take responsibility for how you choose to react, you can do something about the situation. You stop being a victim of the situation or the other person's behavior. Who knows, you might be rushing your sick child to hospital, in which case you will probably still hustle and harry from behind. On the other hand, and more likely in our experience, you realize that you are not actually in that much of a hurry and decide to relax a little. Suddenly the pressure is off and the driver in front didn't even do a thing. All of this hassle was caused by your lack of self-awareness and the inability to let go of your habitual behavior.

Of course, you could continue to drive along feeling frustrated and complaining to yourself that there is nothing you can do to make the person in front go a little faster. Nothing would change and all your complaining and expenditure of emotional energy would get you nowhere. The point is that you do have a choice and it is in exercising this choice that you have the power to change things. If you know that you are in the habit of being in a hurry, you will be able to recognize that your frustration is merely a signpost that says "there is a better way and you have a choice." If you have also taken the time to spell out exactly you want, perhaps something like "I can feel relaxed when I don't get things my own way," you will have the opportunity to make that choice.

BLAME DESTROYS POWER

One of the greatest barriers to change and one of the main reasons that many people feel powerless is because they insist on assigning blame for the problems they face. Rather than ask "What can I do?" their question is "Who is at fault here?" Blame stops us from learning and is a huge roadblock in the way of personal and organizational change.

Blame places the cause of our problems outside ourselves, but by doing so it also places the power to change things with others. This might make us feel better temporarily by pandering to our emotional need to be right, or at least "not wrong," but it doesn't help us change anything. Placing blame lets us continue in the illusion that our hidden rules are still the right rules. In effect, blame is the equivalent of saying: "There is a problem here, but the fault is out there somewhere." Responsibility means taking the attitude that, whatever problem arises, the question I will ask myself is: "What can I do now to take responsibility for getting the results I want?"

> The main reason many people feel powerless is that they insist on assigning blame for the problems they face

This can be an odd piece of wisdom to accept at first. It seems somehow counterintuitive. Surely not every problem we face can be of our own making? We remember one client who was describing a conflict he had with a "difficult" colleague. The two of them did not see eye to eye and tended to argue about even the most trivial decision. At one point in the conversation, when we were discussing the habit of blame, he exclaimed, "But if this situation is not his fault, that means it's my fault and that just isn't right!" Thinking in terms of blame and fault doesn't lead to action and diminishes the likelihood that we will see an opportunity to make a breakthrough.

Efforts to deal with difficulties fail almost immediately if they descend into the question of whose fault it is that there is a difficulty in the first place. Unless the habit of blame is very firmly "outed," when there is a difficulty there will be only two things we can agree on: someone is to blame and it isn't me. The language of blame has an extraordinary capacity to stop people acting and to destroy trust.

We worked with one team in part of a government agency that had what many of the staff called a "blame culture." There was an unusual lack of authenticity between people. When a difficulty arose they would rarely address their concerns directly with those involved, but rather would make obscure comments to shield themselves from any responsibility for what had happened. People found it very difficult to be direct with each other or have an open and honest discussion about areas of disagreement. The atmosphere was stressful and it was almost impossible to make any progress, as people positioned themselves to avoid blame. At least in part, the hidden rules of culture appeared to be something like:

Intention – avoid blame for any problems or difficulties

Awareness – listen for blame or criticism

Action – defend oneself by attributing blame for any problems to others

The challenge was that this culture had existed for so long that people had stopped noticing the subtle ways in which the blame happened. We witnessed many conversations in corridors where the deficiencies of another team were discussed, but rarely saw the same issues raised when the relevant people were there to listen to the comments and take appropriate action. Fortunately, a new chief executive transformed the organization by creating a positive view of how open and honest discussion could facilitate improvement, and enforcing an almost fanatical intolerance of any kind of bad-mouthing.

The tendency to blame is so much of a habit that very few people are aware they have it until it is pointed out to them. But where do you look for the answers to your problems? If you are like nine out of ten of the people we come across, you look outside of yourself. It is the rare soul who admits: "I felt angry because I like to get my own way."

TRY THIS: AN END TO BLAME

Think about someone you don't get along with.
Write about some of the reasons you don't like them.
Think of some specific situations where you didn't
like their behavior. Don't hold back, write what you
really think.

When you have finished, go through what you have
written with a highlighter and mark any statement that
blames the other person for anything you don't like.

Can you think of a different way of looking at the
situation that gives you back your power to choose
your response?

THE UNCONTROLLABLE UNIVERSE

Saying "the problem is out there" is like looking out of the window
and saying, "The roof is leaking because it's raining." While there may
be some literal truth in the statement, it's a very limited truth at best.
It's the truth based on the external circumstances alone. It doesn't take
into account your own response to those circumstances. There is no
use in blaming the rain if you are getting wet; better to look at your
own behavior and notice that there's a hole in the roof you haven't got
around to mending yet. That is a more useful truth. After all, you can
mend the roof but you can't stop the rain from raining.

Think about the implications if your problems, your difficulties, your
frustrations *are* entirely beyond your influence to change. If slow drivers and insensitive bosses really can make your life a misery, isn't this
some kind of hell? Doesn't it mean that the whole universe has to line
itself up just for you to be happy and successful? Is it really likely that
you'll go through life without ever meeting someone who rubs you up
the wrong way, or being confronted with a situation that challenges
your rules? And what if the universe did conspire to let you have things
all your own way? That works for you, but what about everyone else?

153

Does your utopia mean that the rest should be condemned to misery? Let's hope not!

GIVE UP BLAME

What is most important is to take back the power that blame destroys. We can do this by recognizing that we have the power to change and that we exercise that power by taking responsibility for our choices. No matter what the circumstances, whenever we are dissatisfied and want to change things, we need to ask: "What can I do to change this situation?" We can

Blame destroys power, responsibility creates power

help ourselves loosen the hold that the natural tendency to blame has over us by turning within, and seeing that many of the challenges we face are prolonged by our own attachment to playing the game of life in a particular way. When we see this, it frees us up to act in ways that we simply cannot do if we are in the habit of blaming. When we give up the habit of blame we take a great step to becoming "response-able," able to respond to whatever challenges we face. Blame destroys power, responsibility creates power.

The first time we step outside the boundaries of our habitual patterns of thinking is by far the scariest. Living with the language of blame can create all kinds of natural defenses. If the organization you work in has a blame culture, giving up blame can seem a lonely path to tread. Quite naturally, if everyone else asks "Whose fault is it?" when there's a problem, it can be difficult to resist the temptation to join in or get sucked into defending your own role. But there is another way. Turn the question around and ask: "What can I (or we) do now to move things forward?"

You might be tempted to look at what we are suggesting as idealistic. Think of it as a little like one of those theme park rides, with a loop-the-loop and perhaps a twist thrown in for good measure. You stand and look at it from the ground and think, "That can't be safe." But somehow you're persuaded to give it a try, and you find to your astonishment that you don't fall out after all. In fact it's quite exhilarating, so you give it another go. The more you ride, the more confidence you have.

It's the same with giving up the habit of blame. The first time you let go and try something new, you fear that your whole world might collapse. It just doesn't feel right. You kick and scream for a while, but hopefully you are persuaded to try something new by others or through your own growing self-awareness. And of course, the world doesn't come tumbling down around your ears. All that is shattered is the illusion that the way you're seeing things is the only way.

What a wonderful relief it is to stop blaming, to stop playing the victim. You cannot tell the rain to stop, but you can mend the hole in the roof. You cannot avoid coming across people and situations that you find difficult, but you can choose to let go of your habitual patterns of thought and behavior. You cannot choose or control the difficulties you will face, but you can choose how you react to these difficulties.

CONTROL, INFLUENCE, ACCEPT

To give up blame and take responsibility is to acknowledge that there is always something you can do. You never have to accept the illusion that you are powerless in the face of circumstances or other people's behavior. You need to find the personal response, the change in your own behavior, that will lead to a different result.

So what can you do? The answer to this question comes in three parts. There are some things that you can *control,* some things that you can *influence,* and some things that you would be wise to *accept.* Understanding these elements can help you focus your actions in the right place.

CONTROL YOUR RESPONSE

The French philosopher Jean-Paul Sartre said that man is the sum of his actions. Yet it is not only what has happened in the past that determines our future, it is our choices in the here and now that can make the difference. We can't control what has happened in the past, it has already gone. We can't control how things turn out, either. There are so many people and other factors that also contribute to the future. Neither can we control how other people behave. The only thing we truly control is how we respond, what we think, what we say, and what we do.

The driver in our example can't control the speed of the driver in front, but he can control his own speed and how he reacts to what is happening around him. If he gets angry, he may not realize it, but it is his choice to feel like that. He can choose to slow down and relax or he can choose to set out earlier if he really can't afford to be late.

Even when there seem to be no practical actions we can take, we can always choose our internal reaction. No matter how difficult the situation, we can let go of our habitual emotional response. Victor Frankl, who survived a Nazi concentration camp, described this ability to decide our attitude as "the last of the human freedoms," the only thing that cannot be taken away from us, even in the most dreadful circumstances. For Frankl and some of his fellow prisoners, this meant choosing not to give in to hatred of the prison guards. He could have allowed his thoughts to dwell on the horrors he experienced and to grow into hatred. Instead, he chose to forgive. Few of us will ever encounter a situation as terrible as concentration camp prisoners faced. If Frankl can let go of that, then we have no excuse for indulging in disempowering and negative thoughts in a situation we don't like. We can choose to find a more empowering way to respond. Interestingly, Frankl recognized the importance of personal responsibility and proposed that there should be a Statue of Responsibility on the west coast of the United States to balance the message of the Statue of Liberty on the east coast.

INFLUENCE RESULTS

We can influence the results we achieve by making sure that we have clear goals and by acting in line with those goals. Our choices make a difference to our future. We can use the four Ps to make sure that we can picture the positive, precise possibility we want, but nevertheless, whether things turn out how we want them to depends on a whole range of factors that are beyond our control.

We can also influence other people. If we have the skills we need and a good network of relationships we can have more influence, but we will never be entirely beyond the reach of outside circumstances.

For example, Dawn's intention might be to reduce her workload by saying no to some of her colleagues' more extreme requests, but she can't control their reaction when she does this. No matter what she says they will make their own decisions, although she can influence how they react through her actions. Probably the most powerful way to influence what they do would be to build strong relationships with the people whose cooperation she needs, so that she has the opportunity to influence the requests they make of her team.

ACCEPT REALITY

The only thing we are wise to accept is reality. By accept we don't mean to imply that you passively resign yourself to the current state of affairs. There may be things you are unhappy with, and by all means set goals and identify changes that you want to make. That is what this book is designed to help you do. But there is no point arguing that things are different than they really are or that they *should* be different than they are. What has happened has happened and there is little merit in wasting energy wishing things had turned out differently. You can sometimes achieve more by recognizing those things that you cannot change and using your energy to change what *is* within your control or influence.

You can expand your view of reality by understanding your hidden rules and how they influence what you notice, as we have already outlined. And you can take the time to understand more about how other people see things. But while that changes your view of reality, you can't change reality itself. This might seem entirely obvious, but reflect on the extent to which most people do argue with reality.

On one occasion we were with a client who had just been told that a press release that had been sent out on a major project contained some embarrassing factual errors. She spent the next half hour in conversations with various staff discussing what the press release should have said, what should have happened, and why the document had gone out without approval. None of these conversations changed anything. They simply burned off some of the excess emotional energy from wishing that the incident hadn't happened. She could have better spent that energy asking herself and her team what they could do now and how could they avoid a repeat of the same kind of problem in the future.

Of course, most of us do argue with reality, because we have all these judgments about how things should and shouldn't be. Each hidden rule fences off part of what is, so that what we perceive is not what is real but our story about what is real. These are two different things that sometimes bear only a loose relationship to each other.

In organizations that are stuck, it is often because people do not have the courage to face reality as it is. We were asked to work with the senior management team of one division of a large aerospace company. Everywhere we went, everyone was at great pains to explain to us how successful the division was and why its poor figures were not at all indicative of any problems.

CONTROL, INFLUENCE, ACCEPT:
Control response
Influence results
Accept reality

You didn't have to be a genius to sense the anxiety as they tried to convince themselves of their own story. The challenge for this group was getting to the point where they could have an authentic conversation about their difficulties. They wanted to resist reality at all turns. When one of the less senior managers finally broke ranks and talked about his fears, there was a palpable sense of relief as the façade fell away. Only after that moment of authenticity was a breakthrough possible.

TRY DOING THE OPPOSITE

One surprising side effect of the way our senses are wired up and the tendency to see the problem as "out there" is that we get things the wrong way around. When we are stuck, our hidden rules often drive us toward behavior that achieves the exact opposite of the outcome we want. We can uncover new and potentially beneficial opportunities for action by examining what happens if we do the opposite of what we would normally do or instinctively want to do. For example, Dawn wants to say yes to everyone, but she makes the breakthrough by learning to say no. Teri, who we met in the opening chapter, has a habit of giving answers; the breakthrough for her comes when she learns to listen.

As a guideline, when what you are doing isn't working or when you find yourself blaming others for the difficulties you face, consider doing the opposite of what you would normally do. If you are a naturally decisive person, you might need to adopt an inclusive style in order to make progress. On the other hand, if you are a naturally inclusive person, you might make a breakthrough by becoming more decisive.

This can seem an odd technique, but we have seen people make major breakthroughs in their thinking and their ability to take action once they relinquish their attachment to their own way of doing things.

TRY THIS: DO THE OPPOSITE

Think of some of the things that in your view other people should or shouldn't do. This could be something like "People should to listen to me" or "I want my team to take commitments seriously." Write three or four statements down here.

Examine the opposite of each statement. For example, instead of "People should listen to me," reflect on the thought "I should listen to other people." What if you listened? Would there be any merit in that? What if people didn't listen to you? Could that be a good idea? Rather than "I want my team to take our commitments seriously," reflect on the thought "I will take our commitments seriously." What if you did take your commitments more

> seriously? Would that have a positive effect? Is there a way in which you are avoiding your commitments?
>
> Now write down some of the things that you should or shouldn't do, need to or don't need to do. For example, "I need to have the right answer" or "I must always do a great job."
>
> Examine the opposite of each statement. What happens if you think "I don't need to have the right answer?" Are their times when it pays to choose to "not do a great job"?

DO WHAT YOU WANT OTHERS TO DO

One other manifestation of how we get things the wrong way around is that we often find ourselves demanding that other people do exactly what we could usefully do. Those who complain that no one will listen are usually well advised to listen themselves. Those who don't want to be judged would do well to examine how they are judging other people.

This is exactly the case with Eva in Chapter 4, who fears that she will be judged by her peers when she gives a presentation at a major conference. She is, in fact, judging her peers. It's the same with John, whom we met in Chapter 6, who sees people as unfriendly. If he wants them to be friendly he can make a start by being friendly himself. Another way of looking at this is that whatever annoys or frustrates us about other people can be turned around. Rather than talking about what other people should do or should be like, we can examine what *we* should do or what *we* should be like.

Here is a dialogue that illustrates how powerful the idea of doing the opposite can be. This conversation is between Dave and Tara, a middle manager for a large housing group. Tara was responsible for rolling out a new project management system throughout the organization and was having problems getting buy-in from the project managers who needed to implement the approach. She had been chosen for the project because of her knowledge of this type of system and how it could benefit the organization. Dave was asked to help her in advance of a meeting she had planned with the project managers.

Dave: What's your goal? How will you know the meeting has been successful?

Tara: All project managers will buy in to using the system.

Dave: What do you think is getting in the way of that now?

Tara: I don't know. Everyone is supposed to use the system, but only about half of the project managers are using it and some of those aren't entering all the data we need. I've sent them all a full briefing and step-by-step instructions. It's really simple. I don't see what else I could have done to make the system clearer.

Dave: What feedback have you had about what people think of the system?

Tara: Hardly any. Mostly it's just been people asking about things that are already explained in the manual or asking me to enter their data for them. I don't see why they can't simply trust that it will be of benefit to them and use the system as it was intended. If they took the time to understand how it works they would see how it could help.

Dave: How do you feel about that?

Tara: I'm really frustrated and a bit annoyed that people won't do what is needed. I've tried all kinds of ways of getting across to people the benefits of this solution, but they just don't buy it.

Dave: What are you planning to do at the meeting with the project managers?

Tara: I'm not sure there is much more I can do, other than present the message again about what they need to do and the benefits to them of using the system.

Dave: Do you think that will work? It sounds like they've already had that message.

Tara: That's exactly what I'm thinking, but what else can I do?

Dave: Have you thought about doing the opposite of that?

Tara: What do you mean by the opposite? I don't see how not telling them about the benefits is going to help.

Dave: What about taking the time to understand what they have to say about their problems and what they need from the system? What impact do you think that would have?

Tara: That sounds risky. We've spent a lot of time working on this and I don't want to see it fall apart.

Dave: What's the risk? What do you think they might say?

Tara: They might just pick the system to pieces. I don't want the meeting to be negative.

Dave: You said you wanted people to trust that the system would benefit them. What about trusting that what they would have to say will be of positive benefit to you?

Tara: I see what you did there. You turned my statement on its head. That's interesting. But I'm not clear how I would go about doing that.

Dave: There is a simple way of doing this. Ask them two questions: What concerns do they have about the system as it stands and what recommendations do they have for improving it? That way you allow them to get anything that bothers them off their chest, but you also keep the meeting positive. Do you think that would help?

Tara: I can see how that would certainly flush out why they aren't using the system. But what do I do if they recommend something I can't give them?

Dave: Then you tell them. But at least this way you show them that what matters to them matters to you. That's often the best way to get someone's buy-in.

Tara: This sounds interesting. Let's give it a go.

Tara tried the approach she had agreed with Dave and learned a great deal from the meeting. She discovered that the main problem was confusion with how the new project management system related to existing approaches. She was easily able to address these concerns and make a few small changes that gave the project managers what they needed. Tara and her boss were delighted with the result and they adopted the same approach for all future change initiatives.

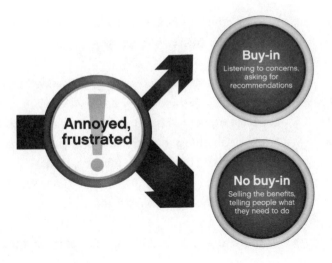

Figure 14   Tara's do-how map

THE HEART OF CHANGE

Realizing that you always have a choice, and then taking responsibility for those choices, lies at the heart of change. You can't control the circumstances you find yourself in or how other people behave, but you can choose how you respond. It is that choice that gives you the power to change anything you want to. You can make it easier to choose by being sensitive to your emotional reactions, being clear about what you want, and being aware of your habitual response. Ultimately, it's when you acknowledge that you can take back the power to choose your own way that the changes you want in your life and your work start to happen.

TRY THIS: YOUR POWER TO CHANGE

Write for 15 minutes about your power to change whatever you want to at work or in your life. Don't edit what you write, just get any thoughts that arise down on paper. Repeat this at least four times over a period of two weeks. You can write on four consecutive nights or once every few days. Don't worry if what you are writing doesn't make sense or contains contradictions. Just write.

Once you have finished writing, go over what you have written. Are there any areas where you perceive a lack of power to change what you want to change? Look for anything that you see as impossible or a "can't do." Challenge such thinking by asking:

- Are these thoughts really true?

- Is there any merit in the opposite of these thoughts?

- What if these things were difficult rather than impossible? What would I do then?

Chapter 8

ORGANIZATIONS CHANGE WHEN PEOPLE CHANGE

How to develop
organizational do-how

Organizations are difficult to change. Clients often engage us because they feel frustrated by the lack of progress in bringing about the changes they want. They may be clear about their strategy and their objectives, but something keeps getting in the way of real change happening. Restructuring, often the first approach companies turn to in times of change, moves people on the organizational chart, but they are still the same people and if they work in the same way they will get largely the same results. It is similar with approaches driven by rewritten policies and procedures or the launch of a new corporate vision and values. These can help to create the fertile ground for change, but they rarely produce much difference on their own.

The most powerful driver of change is a visible shift in the behavior of key individuals

Many people see personal change and organizational change as two different issues, but in truth, personal change is the foundation on which organizational change is built. In our experience, the most powerful driver of change, and the only thing that brings about lasting cultural change, is a visible shift in the behavior of key individuals that is consistent with the overall direction the organization is seeking to take. The more senior and influential the person is, the more important it is that they are seen to model behavior that is in line with where the organization is going rather than where it has come from. Without this genuine shift in the way individuals work, any broader efforts to communicate and implement change will be confused at best. While organizational change may start with vision and must be followed through with powerful communication, it is ultimately the sum of personal behavioral changes that leads to the desired breakthrough in performance.

There are some huge challenges in developing buy-in to change and building an atmosphere of trust where people work together toward a common aim, but that's a whole other problem. We are not talking here about how we enroll people into what the organization wants from them. We spend a lot of time with people who really buy in to change and might even have worked out what changes they want to make, but somehow, despite their commitment, they have the same conversations, behave in the same way, and nothing new happens.

HOW WE WORK AROUND HERE

So what are the inch-thick chains that anchor organizational performance to the past? The answer, of course, is culture. There is a direct parallel between how people change and how teams and organizations change. Just as people have hidden rules that are the source of their success but also limit them, organizations and individual teams have culture. Organizational culture is sometimes described as "the way we do things around here" and it has the same qualities as hidden rules. Culture defines the rules of success in any given organization and these rules become hidden in plain sight, just like an individual's hidden rules. In reality the culture of an organization is no more hidden than habitual behavior is, except that it becomes invisible to anyone who is immersed in that culture for long enough. What is hidden is the fact that people are unconsciously choosing one way of behaving when there are many other possible ways.

Anyone new to the culture will soon see the particular modes of operating in that organization or team. It can be difficult to adjust to a different culture when joining a new organization. In large organizations there can be considerable variation in the nuances of the culture across different departments and teams. Nevertheless, even the largest businesses we have worked with have some strong common elements to their culture that run across very diverse functions and multiple locations.

One should never underestimate the power of culture, both as a positive force for transmitting and sustaining the values of the business and as a brake on necessary change. It is the culture that helps align diverse people with a wide range of backgrounds, expertise, and skills and gets them working together toward common aims. It is also culture that can stifle new ways of working and

Never underestimate the power of culture

undermine efforts to adapt to changing circumstances. The challenge for any organization that wants to implement change is to recognize the difference between those changes that the current culture supports and change that requires a different way of thinking and working. The former will usually be much more straightforward, whereas the latter will be difficult and require an entirely different approach.

ORGANIZATIONAL DO-HOW

Strategy and culture cannot be treated separately. If strategy is about what the organization wants to achieve and the things it must do to reach those aims, culture is about how people work and the way they behave. A company that wants to change the results it obtains needs to make sure that its culture is aligned with its strategy. This is what we call organizational do-how. Organizational do-how is an organization's capacity to act in a way that is consistent with its stated aims.

Aside from the broader issue of developing trust, the do-how map is the starting point for developing organizational do-how. By creating a clear distinction between the way we want people to think and behave and how the culture currently leads them to think and behave, we can open up the choice that leads to do-how. The times when people are acting out of negative or uncomfortable emotions point to do-how moments, when the choices that those individuals make can either reinforce the old story of where the organization has come from, or bring to life the new story of where it is heading. It still takes courage and emotional maturity to make those choices, but if enough people choose the upward fork, change begins to happen.

For example, if we want to create a culture where people are customer focused, we need to spell out what precisely it means to be customer focused in terms of specific behaviors and ways of thinking. The more vividly we can bring this to life and help people in the organization picture what it looks like, the more likely it is that they will behave that way. However, that's not enough. If a company takes the trouble to put precious resources into creating a customer-focused culture, there is a good chance that the culture isn't customer focused at the moment. So while the company can put up posters exhorting everyone to listen to customers' needs, the chances are that this will have little impact. Even if it invests in training, much of the impact will be lost as the old culture reasserts itself. We need to identify what the downward fork looks like and make sure that there is a strong awareness of what specific behaviors and ways of thinking the organization wants to drop. Then there will be some specific moments or situations when the choice between the old ways of working and the new can make a significant impact on whether change sticks or fails.

If you look back at the example of the water company in the opening chapter, you can see the choice that some of the senior managers had between behaving in a way that reinforced the old, hierarchical, risk-averse culture and behaving with the lighter touch that allowed managers autonomy to make decisions for themselves. Agreeing that they wanted to make this choice wasn't enough, though. They needed to spot those do-how moments when their emotional reactions pushed them down the downward fork and their intention to create a less hierarchical culture was overridden by their habit of taking responsibility away from managers. The do-how map for this senior management team illustrates a similar pattern to the one we see when looking at individual breakthroughs.

The important thing that helped the team was to draw to their attention that they had a choice and that they were in danger of making that choice not out of intention but out of habit. By highlighting the choices they were making, and looking at the consequences of each option, it was easier for the team to develop the do-how they needed to transform their own fears into a genuine commitment to change.

SPOTTING THE CULTURE

There are many jokes about consultants and we've been on the wrong end of most of them, but one of the reasons consultants can add value is that they aren't immersed in the organizational culture. By asking what seem like simple questions and listening carefully to the answers, it's easy to spot the hidden rules.

169

Figure 15   Team do-how map

The approach is the same as uncovering an individual's hidden rules. You can look at what makes people in the organization uncomfortable and what the organization is trying to avoid to get a good idea of the negative aspects of the current culture; you can consider the organization's strengths to see where its limitations might lie.

What is most important is to listen. The culture is only hidden because people have stopped noticing that the choices they are making are in fact choices. By simply listening to what people talk about and what they don't talk about, it's easy to tune into the hidden rules that describe the culture. People who are new to the organization and mavericks who refuse to fit in with the way it works are also a good source of insight.

STAGES OF ORGANIZATIONAL MATURITY

In the same way that our personal hidden rules make sense within our own narrative or story of how the world works, so organizational culture makes sense of that organization's story of how the world works. When we work with an organization we try to understand its unique story, but over many years we have noticed that there are some common patterns to the way the story and culture develop, particularly in large and mature organizations. There are three specific stages that we come across again and again. Each stage has its strengths, what it brings to the organization. However, over time these strengths can limit the capacity to grow and take on new challenges or more effective ways of working. What started as a strength begins to hold the organization back and its performance slowly falls off, as seen in each curve of Figure 16. If the organization gets stuck at a particular developmental stage, the role of senior management is to get it onto a new upward track. Each stage of cultural development builds on or includes the strengths of the previous stage and transcends it by introducing new approaches that deal with its limitations. In our experience, an organization can make a transition from one stage to the next, but it can't skip a step in between.

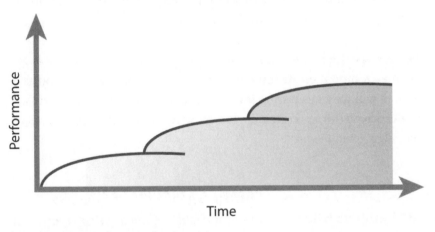

Figure 16 Stages of organizational maturity

The transitions that many senior executives are wrestling with are those from "conformance" to "achievement," then from "achievement" to "collaboration." The main strengths of a conformance culture are that it is very good at laying down rules and processes to make sure everything runs smoothly. Any organization needs rules and processes, but in a conformance culture these can seem more important than customers and results. The underlying message of such a culture is that it's safer to "not get anything wrong" than to "get things right." In this kind of organization people who are more comfortable with following procedures are the ones who thrive. This stifles creativity and innovation, meaning that change and improvement are slow and difficult to implement. The natural next step is to create a culture where people focus on results and challenge the way things are done in order to improve performance, which we call an "achievement culture." This is the transition that the water company we described earlier was in the progress of making.

Over time, a culture focused on achievement can also become a limitation if people focus on results only for their own team or department, at the expense of the bigger picture for the whole organization. The next step culturally is for people and teams to work together across boundaries to challenge and improve the way things are done, guided by clear goals and a desire to get the best results. We call this a collaborative or high-performance culture. Many of our larger clients with headcounts in the thousands wrestle with this transition.

We can see here the organizational equivalent of "Every strength becomes a limitation in some circumstances." Great systems and procedures will inevitably stifle innovation and creativity. People who are results driven can, and often do, get in the way of collaboration between individuals and teams.

CREATING A PICTURE OF SUCCESS

Change happens when people see that what they will gain is of greater value than the old story promises

Cultural change happens when people see that what they will gain from the change is of greater value than what is promised by the old story embedded in the existing culture. The rules or culture don't spring out of thin air, but are a response to circumstances the company finds itself in and the results it is committed to achieving. The culture makes sense given the organizational story. That is why one of the most important roles of any leader or agent of change is as a storyteller. The point of the story is to create a new picture of success for the organization that people can reorientate themselves with.

When there is a need for significant change, a real sense of confusion can arise. We often meet people who tell us, "But we are good at what we do, why do we need to change?" People have an inbuilt need for what they are doing to make sense and to leave them feeling positive about their contribution.

Creating and telling a compelling and positive story for the organization is one of the absolutely essential ingredients if you want to generate wider buy-in to change. The new culture then flows naturally from the story and helps people make sense of why they need to change.

One of our oldest clients moved to become chief executive of a complex group of service businesses. He had made his reputation at a similar company that had been on its knees, radically restructuring and shedding nearly half the workforce, but transforming its fortunes. In his new role he struggled to find the same impetus. The organization was reasonably well run and was making good returns. He confided in us:

> "It was easier in a failing business. Everyone could see what the situation was, so anything we came up with was accepted, no matter how radical. The need for change made sense to people. The new business is in good shape but I want it to be a great business. It's difficult to sell the idea of change to people who already see themselves as successful. People have too much to lose. Without a compelling reason to change there is more resistance."

The three Rs can provide a great starting point for creating a compelling organizational story. Start by figuring out what your message is regarding the results that change will deliver. Ask yourself whether this is compelling. Will it speak to the needs and concerns of the people whose buy-in you need? Most people don't like change and will have to see that it will deliver something important to them if they are to give their full commitment. Next, consider the current reality. What is working well that you want to acknowledge and what are the problems or challenges that the change will address? Will the changes you are planning address the day-to-day frustrations that people experience? If not, they will wonder why they are bothering with the effort the change requires. Finally, set out clearly what will be expected from people, being as precise as you can. Illustrate a few specific behavioral changes and give examples of what the new way of working looks like.

For example, we worked with an IT services company to develop a new approach to its training and consultancy business. Its change story went something like this:

⟫ **Result** – we want to be seen as the company to go to for a total solution around IT services. This means that we provide solutions to the people problems around IT as well as the technical solutions. Our focus will be on making the customer's IT team work well, as opposed to simply making their technology work.

⟫ **Reality** – our marketplace has become commoditized. There are many larger IT training companies that can provide training profitably at a lower cost than us. Most customers make spending decisions based on price before quality or impact. We are losing customers where we compete on price alone. We win and retain customers where we can add value by providing a tailored solution to the wider problem of making IT teams work effectively.

⟫ **Response** – we will identify the customers' broader needs rather than merely their IT training requirements. We will pay attention to the people issues and the way IT staff work as a team.

This might seem like a fairly simple story, but the effect on the organization was dramatic. Where previously sales staff had felt beleaguered by continual downward pressure on prices, they now had a clear story to tell their customers, one that set them apart from their competitors.

TRY THIS: YOUR CHANGE STORY

Think of a change you are planning in your organization or team. Use the three Rs to tell the change story:

- How do you want things to be as a **result** of the change? What impact do you want the change to make? What will the benefits be when you are successful with the change?

- What are the key facts about your current **reality** that everyone needs to understand? What is driving the change? What will the consequences be if you don't change?

- What is actually going to change? What **response** do you expect from people? What will they need to do or stop doing? How do you want them to behave?

LISTENING AND COMMUNICATION

In any organization where we have worked to help create significant change, there is one word that comes up every time: communication. When people talk about problems with communication, they almost always mean a *lack* of communication; very often their dissatisfaction is that they don't feel they are being listened to. Effective communication is always two way.

In our experience, the most effective change programs start with listening. Listen to what people's ambitions are and what bugs them about the way things are now and you are halfway to success. Staff may not always know what the solutions are, but they certainly know what the problems are. Any change program that solves the problems people grapple with day to day, as they see them, will gain wide support. If the change story becomes *our* story rather than *your* story, it is much more

175

likely to gain traction. Don't even try to communicate the new story until you have listened to what the mass of people in the organization are saying. This is not difficult to do, but is often forgotten.

Listening and being seen to listen are some of the best ways to generate buy-in to change

Communication is what tells the story of the organization. It is what joins people together and allows them to see where they fit. Never underestimate the level and volume of communication that are needed to embed the new story. Everything in an organization communicates the culture: the conversations people have, the way meetings are run, how budgets are set, HR policies, the type of performance appraisals people receive, even the way offices are laid out. Trying to introduce new ideas around culture and behavior is like trying to launch a new brand of cola. The existing brands have a great deal of recognition and the change inevitably meets with resistance.

When talking about the new organizational story, the best storytellers demonstrate the three Cs of communication:

⟶ They are **clear**. The story they tell makes sense and relates to the reality that people experience around them. They use language that people recognize and adapt that language to their audience. They use multiple channels such as direct conversation, blogs, posters, screensavers, and team briefings to get their message across in a wide variety of ways. They tell memorable stories that make sense of why change is happening, what it will deliver, and what it means for individuals in practice.

⟶ They are **concise**. They never try to get more than five or six points across at a time. They use simple examples that emphasize what they want from people. They find simple ways to help others remember what they have said.

⟶ They are **consistent**. They repeat their messages again and again using the same key words and images. They never assume that simply because someone may have heard the same message before, they don't need to hear it again. The message they communicate through their spoken and written words is backed up by their own behavior. They give the listener confidence that the message is here to stay and can't be ignored.

This last point is particularly important. Many people are skeptical about change and will wait to see if it's for real before they commit their own time and energy to help make it happen. So many organizational change initiatives come and go without any real impact that, sadly, it can be a sensible strategy to ignore a change program. Consistent, repeated messages over a period of time make the messages impossible to avoid or ignore and overcome this inertia.

HOW YOU BEHAVE TELLS THE STORY

It can sometimes be difficult to get the message across about the changes you want to make in your team or organization. You might, for example, tell people that you want them to prioritize or be more customer focused or whatever else is going to help you get the results you need. But *telling* people what you want rarely helps them change. So

> **The most powerful form of communication is what you do and how you behave**

how can you communicate those important shifts in behavior that can make the difference between success and failure?

What the most effective leaders have always understood is that the most powerful form of communication is what you do and how you behave. Most people will pay more attention to what you do than what you say. The way you behave communicates to those around you, particularly those who look to you for guidance. There is no day off from this role if you are in a position of authority or leadership. If your behavior models the old ways of working that are holding the organization back, you will be in danger of sending conflicting messages. The places where leaders have been most effective at making change happen are those where senior people's verbal and written messages are entirely matched by their behavioral messages.

We worked with one local council that had a reputation for being dreadfully old-fashioned and resistant to change. Everything about the organization spoke of complacency and stagnation. It was more like a museum than a workplace.

We had been asked by the new chief executive to work with the senior team to create a vision for the organization, one that was dynamic, professional, and high performing. It was an uphill struggle. The story among many of the people who worked there, including some of the senior managers, was "nothing ever changes, it's not possible to change, and even if we tried to change anything we'd be stopped."

The council had been formed during a reorganization of local government and outside one of the offices stood a brass sign bearing the name of the previous town corporation. The chief executive asked staff about the sign. "We asked for it to be changed but nobody ever came," was the reply.

"Just wait here a moment," he said. He went back through the main doors, only to reappear about ten minutes later, brass sign in one hand and screwdriver in the other. "I'll leave the screwdriver here in case there's anything else you want to change," he added. The message was clear and well understood by everyone who heard the tale.

This "brass plaque moment" swept through the organization like wildfire. People started clearing out cupboards and ripping down yellowed posters that no longer had any meaning or relevance. Whole teams organized clear-it-out Fridays and move-it Mondays. This physical clearout was accompanied by a mental clearout as they realized that anything was possible and the senior team started to take responsibility for reinventing the organization. Many other things led to the change that now took off across all parts of the business, and good communications and a leadership development program helped, but this one simple act more than any other crystallized the chief executive's message.

FOCUS ON THE POSITIVE

Focusing on what you want to avoid can be a useful short-term strategy in a crisis, but it is energy sapping in the longer term. Whatever story you tell, whatever picture you paint, it will be successful to the extent that it gets across the message about what you want and motivates people to get involved.

We once worked with a photographic supplies business with a multi-million turnover that had a negative atmosphere of fear and distrust between its senior executives and the bulk of the workforce. The business had been through a tough time in a recession and had had to lay off nearly 10 percent of its workforce. When we listened to what people talked about, they focused almost entirely on saving money and balancing the budget. While this was a natural response to the austerity four years earlier, it was sustaining the negative atmosphere and people felt little enthusiasm for the changes the senior management were planning. In addition, the senior executives were defensive and this further undermined trust.

With the senior team, we created a new story around how the company spent its money to develop new markets and deliver an even better service for its customers. This led to a much more positive story about what the company wanted to *achieve*, rather than what it wanted to *avoid*. It took time to rebuild trust, but eventually the new story took hold and people started to get excited about the future again.

THE POWER OF PRECISION

Precise language has the power to contribute to a breakthrough. This is demonstrated by a meeting we had with a working group from the Organisation for Economic Co-operation and Development (OECD) that was developing guidance on creating sustainable cities. The group involved 27 country representatives plus their support staff and had met on a number of occasions for up to three days at a time. They were struggling to come to a consensus on what should be in the guidance and needed a breakthrough.

Our first question was what precisely they meant by a "sustainable city." This was met with considerable resistance. We were told that the answer was obvious and that we should not waste the group's time with such trivial questions. Knowing how important precision is, particularly with such a vague term as "sustainable cities," we persevered and asked each participant to write down their own definition of what they meant by a sustainable city. There were 27 participants and we received 28 unique answers, since one participant insisted on giving two responses. The participants were shocked. How could something that they felt to be so obvious cause such confusion? Following further reflection and discussion, the group realized that there were two distinct dimensions to the challenge of creating a sustainable city: what they came to call sectoral skills (building roads, sewers, houses, etc.) and integrating processes (organizing government, developing a system of law, creating a free press, etc.). This tension is what had divided the group up until that point. They now saw that they were talking across different but complementary aspects of the same problem. They had made a breakthrough and they could see a way forward.

LET THE MAVERICKS TELL YOU WHAT IS POSSIBLE

In a large organization it is often not that difficult to identify what the upward fork looks like. The large number of people involved means that there will inevitably be a wide range of approaches and styles of working. Most people will gravitate around the cultural norms, but there will be others who do things their own way. Many of these will be people whose focus is on finding ways around the rules to make great things happen. They can be seen as mavericks, especially in a conformance culture, but in our experience many of the best ideas come from people who refuse to rigidly follow the rules.

We are not suggesting that anarchy be allowed to reign. It's just that when individuals bump up against the limitations of the current cultural norms, there will be some who simply yield to the pressure to conform, and others who find ways around the rules and make things work in spite of the culture. These mavericks can be an incredibly fertile source of new ways of working when the organization needs to change. They are often the people who are at the cutting edge of getting the organization onto the new and emerging cultural curve. They refuse to be told "that's impossible" and point to what is really possible if you are willing to break a few cultural rules. They may well be seen as negative or difficult by some but, if they have energy, that energy can be channeled into finding positive ways forward for the business. Discover what they are doing and nurture it.

TRUST AND RESPONSIBILITY

In an organization without trust, change is almost impossible. Without trust, everyone wants to know all the details for all the wrong reasons. Making simple decisions takes an age and the decisions that are made get unmade as people maneuver for their agenda to be noticed. Without trust, it is difficult to learn or try new things, as any small mistake is pounced on. Nobody wants to take responsibility for difficult decisions or new ways of doing things.

What tends to be called a "blame culture" is a symptom of low levels of trust. People focus on "Who is at fault?" rather than "What can we learn?" and "What can we do now to move forward?" This disempowers the whole organization. A blame culture is the organizational equivalent of saying "there's nothing I can do" as people jockey to pass responsibility on to others and play it safe by sticking to well-worn ways of working.

On the other hand, when levels of trust are high, people are more willing to learn and receive feedback about the areas they might need to develop. They are also more likely to try new approaches and to take responsibility for finding new solutions when problems arise. Thus a culture of trust underpins organizational do-how.

To answer the question of how to build trust fully is well beyond the scope of this book, but suffice it to say that if there is no trust at the outset, then the most important role for any leader is to create it. The key is to remember that the ends must be embedded in the means. If you want to create a culture of trust, you have to behave in a way that is worthy of trust and that communicates trust. This means driving out blame, enabling people to have open and honest conversations about what they are dissatisfied with, listening to the needs and concerns of people who are struggling with change, encouraging people to try new ways of working, and seeing any setback as an opportunity to learn. There are simple ways of building trust and driving out blame that take time and commitment but yield results. While there are no quick fixes in building trust, it can be done if the commitment exists to do so.

FIRST LOOK IN THE MIRROR

If you want to change your team or your business or even just some aspect of your life, first look in the mirror. The culture of an organization will usually reflect the hidden rules of the most senior people in the business, particularly if they have been around for a long time. It can be almost impossible to bring about changes in the culture unless this is addressed by the most senior people. This often means the chief executive taking a long, hard look at his or her own ways of thinking and behaving.

> If you want to change your team or your business or even just some aspect of your life, first look in the mirror

We witnessed this problem at first hand when we worked with Johan, who had built from scratch a small group of environmental businesses mainly involved in recycling or home improvements and employing over 500 people. Johan wanted to back off from the day-to-day running of the business and had been trying for over ten years to recruit a strong management team that could keep things moving while he worked on other projects. He wanted other people to take more responsibility for making decisions. The problem for Johan was that, despite employing well-paid recruitment consultants and using industry best-practice recruitment processes, the managers he hired never lived up to his standards and often left within a year of joining. No matter what he tried, he couldn't establish a stable, working management team and felt shackled to the business, the only person who could provide the necessary leadership.

Johan asked us to work with his management team to help establish the leadership behaviors he wanted to see from them. It soon became very apparent to us that the challenge was to get him to examine his own behavior. It was clear to everyone around Johan that his story was something along the lines of: "Everyone is incompetent and I always have to step in and rescue them." This manifested itself as Johan taking control of almost every detail of the business, even getting involved in decisions about what brand of coffee to buy for the mess room.

We heard numerous stories of the same pattern repeated again and again. Johan would recruit a seemingly competent manager with the appropriate qualifications and experience. If they were of a compliant nature, he would tell them what to do but then complain when they failed to take decisions for themselves, since this, he said, is what he wanted from them. He would often end up firing people like this as they failed to live up to his standards. On the other hand, there were some more decisive managers who had ideas of their own. These he clashed with when they resisted his constant meddling in the details he had asked them to manage. They frequently left as they found the stress of battling with an interfering boss too much. It was an impossible situation. Johan wanted to recruit decisive people in his own image, but the reality was that he could only work with people who would agree with his decisions and they didn't live up his standards. Over a period of ten years, he recruited or promoted and then lost or demoted more managers than a company five times larger and still didn't have a stable and effective management team.

The challenge was that Johan had never examined his own ways of thinking and behaving and how these had created the organizational culture. He saw his behavior as "normal," viewed through the lens of his own hidden rules. He was focusing on solving a problem with his managers when he needed to look at his own behavior.

We reflected back to Johan what we were seeing and what we had heard throughout the business. "You're suggesting I'm the problem?" he asked. We weren't too sure we were going to get invited back after that.

We did hear from him after a couple of weeks, when he emailed to say he wanted to meet at his home. He confided in us, "I thought you two had lost it when we last met, but since then I've taken a long, hard look in the mirror." Despite wanting to blame us for telling him some difficult truths, he had the courage to look at himself and take responsibility for what had happened and what now needed to be done. He became intrigued by the idea that what he saw as his strengths were also the source of the limitations he was now bumping up against. Over the next few months, he worked hard to understand how he could modify his behavior to get the best out of the people around him. He made a breakthrough and to this day he still uses the phrase: "If you have a problem, first look in the mirror."

ORGANIZATIONAL CHANGE IS PERSONAL CHANGE

Organizations make breakthroughs when people make breakthroughs. There are some added dimensions, particularly around trust and communication, but the most powerful driver of change is a visible shift in the behavior of key individuals. The more senior and influential the person is, the more important it is that they are seen to model behavior that is in line with where the organization is going, rather than where it has come from. When this shift in the way individuals work is made, it is the most powerful form of communication and builds trust that change is real and cannot be ignored. There is no substitute for personal behavioral changes consistent with the breakthrough in performance that the organization wants to make.

> Organizations make breakthroughs when people make breakthroughs

TRY THIS: YOUR ORGANIZATION'S HIDDEN RULES
What is the culture in your organization?

- **Intention** – what is the implicit goal of people in the company? This is unlikely to be as simple as making a profit. Listen to the stories that people tell.

- **Awareness** – what do people pay attention to? What information seems important to them?

- **Action** – what do people habitually do? What do they habitually avoid?

Chapter 9

USING THE DO-HOW MAP

From adversity to advantage

There is an old joke about a man who is out hiking in the countryside and gets lost. He stops at a crossroads to ask the way of two locals who are chewing the fat over a farm gate. "Do you know the way to the Red Lion Inn?" he asks. The locals start debating with each other in a dialect he can barely understand. The first is gesticulating in one direction, while the other is shaking his head and keeps pointing vigorously in another direction. After a while, the man interrupts their deliberations to say, "If you aren't sure of the way that's fine." "No, no, no, no, no, no. We knows where it is," one of them replies. "It's just that if we were going there we wouldn't start from here."

You can use any adversity as the starting point for a breakthrough

START WHERE YOU ARE

When they need a breakthrough people often wonder where to start, but we want you to know that you can start from anywhere. If you have a clear goal that's a great place to begin, but more often all you have is a state of confusion and frustration. You don't know what you want. You simply know that there is something you are not happy with or can't make progress with. You don't have to see that as a problem, though. You can use any adversity as the starting point for a breakthrough, turning adversity to advantage. When you recognize that the negative emotions you experience point to the choices you have, you can use that insight to lead you to a breakthrough. Necessity may be the mother of invention, but dissatisfaction is the father of most breakthroughs.

Whenever you feel stuck, ask yourself: "How do I want things to be?"

This is especially important to remember when working with a group or team. Creating a clear shared goal can be very difficult. The likelihood that people will experience negative emotions is very high. When you experience difficulty or disagreement, it can be easy to see other people as the problem. This can lead down a blind alley, as the instinct to blame leaves people feeling powerless and gives the illusion that a breakthrough isn't possible. That is why it is useful to see that any difficulty, or adversity, can be transformed into a potential advantage by asking: "How do we want things to be?"

THE THREE RS AND THE DO HOW MAP

We can use the three Rs to map out the changes we want to make. This is a deceptively simple but very powerful way to organize our thoughts. It invites us to ask how we want things to be, how things are now, and what we need to do to move toward our goal.

Even when we are armed with that knowledge, however, we don't always do what we know will work. Our habitual behavior is simply too strong. For example, we might know that we need to listen to gain the trust of other people, but we don't listen because we are in the habit of talking. Or, even if we know that we need to spend more time planning before diving into action, we are hijacked by our hidden rules and off we go without a thought. The challenge is that our hidden rules determine how we look at problems and what breakthroughs seem possible. When we are stuck, it can be difficult to see a way forward as our patterns of thought take us around the same loops again and again.

That's why we need the do-how map. The three Rs help us figure out what to do; the do-how map helps us break free from our habits and actually do it. Using organizational language, the three Rs help us to develop our strategy, but the do-how map helps us to change the culture.

The three Rs help to develop the strategy, the do-how map helps to change the culture

HIDDEN RULES AND THE THREE RS

We sometimes describe the three Rs as the three rules of success; if you prefer, you can think of them as the different strokes you need to play a sport well. For example, if you want to be really good at golf, you need a good drive so that you can hit the ball a long way, a good short game so that you can get out of bunkers, and the ability to putt the ball once you are on the green. If you emphasize any two of these and neglect the third, you might be a good golfer but you are unlikely to be a truly great golfer. You might get on the green in two strokes but then take three or four strokes to putt the ball; or if you slice every ball off the tee, it is unlikely that your putting will make up for it.

One of the reasons the three Rs are so powerful is that they force us to ask questions that challenge our habitual ways of thinking. Each element of the three Rs requires us to exercise a different capacity and ask a different set of questions. This is where the three Rs and the do-how map come together. Understanding what the *reality* of a situation is requires awareness and isn't the same as deciding what your goals are, which requires intention. The questions you might ask to clarify the *results* you want are not the same as the questions you would ask to determine the best *response* to a given situation. Yet, in our experience, these three forms of inquiry get muddled up, so that most people's thinking in this area is fuzzy and incomplete. This is because their hidden rules don't allow them to exercise one or more of the three capacities: they don't use their *intention* to set goals, they don't use their *awareness* to get a deeper understanding of what is going on, and they don't choose their *actions*.

Many people fail to set goals. They keep themselves busy reacting to whatever problems come up, but they don't take hold of the situation and determine how they want things to be. They can be very good managers and problem solvers as long as someone else is driving the agenda and setting the goals. They will rarely change anything or create new and innovative ways of doing things unless there is an external drive to do so. For these people, necessity really is the mother of invention. They keep many plates spinning and are admired for their energy, but nothing changes and they fail to provide any real vision. It can take hours of patient listening before moving them on by asking: "So how would you like things to be?" or "What do you want your actions to achieve for you?" It can be difficult for them to set goals because they are so clear that things are the way they are that they lose sight of the possibility that a breakthrough is possible. They end up blown around by whatever events come their way and fail to realize that they could determine their own future.

We also meet people who fail to take the time to understand their reality. While they might be clear about the results they want, they are eager to get into action before they really understand what is going on. People like this make good innovators and usually have lots of drive, but they can fail to take others with them and lack the well-developed capacity for awareness that can pick up on the nuances that really matter. They will take risks and reinvent the wheel because they are shooting from the hip rather than grounding their plans in evidence and data about what works. When they get things right, it looks like genius. When they get stuck, they often repeat the same action over and over again, perplexed as to why their sheer energy doesn't produce the result they want. They can be helped by challenging their assumptions and getting them to focus their awareness on the facts and figures before leaping into action.

Slightly less often, we meet people who fail to get into any action at all. They spend a great deal of time analyzing their reality or daydreaming about how things could be, and they fail to get going and take responsibility for making the changes they want. They have lots of ideas but don't always see them through to fruition. They work well in situations where there is an external discipline that forces them into action or where there is a strong, action-focused team to support their ideas. When people like this get stuck, they either suffer from paralysis by analysis or they want to talk endlessly about their plans or problems without any sense that they need to get on with something and see what happens. They can be moved into action by asking: "So what will you do then?"

By systematically following the three Rs, you can identify the best course of action to make a breakthrough and achieve a better outcome in anything you set your mind to. This is the first step in making a breakthrough. It's common sense, but it's far from common practice. Using the three Rs systematically starts the process of challenging your hidden rules by forcing you to consider questions that normally seem unimportant or too obvious to give any real attention to.

Much of the time, the fact that you might miss out one of the three Rs is fine. Members of a team will play different roles and you might have good people around you who make up for your own shortcomings. It doesn't matter if you never set goals until you find yourself in a role that requires you to set goals to be successful. However, when you are stuck, working systematically through the three Rs so that you are clear what results you want, you understand what the reality is that you are dealing with, and you identify actions that will actually deliver what you want will help you identify the opportunity for a breakthrough.

ASKING THE BREAKTHROUGH QUESTION

One of the things we hope you will do is to start hearing the three Rs come up in conversations. The next time you are in a meeting that's a little boring or are listening to the news on the radio, you might notice many conversations about problems with various people giving their version of the facts (*reality*); or you might hear suggestions and discussion about what might be done (*response*); or there might even be some ideas about the difference that will be made or the outcome that will be achieved as a consequence of those actions (*result*). The chances are that you will hear one or two of the three Rs but not all three. Whichever one is missing, you can be sure that asking the question that focuses attention on that area will help people move toward a breakthrough.

The three Rs give people a language to organize their thoughts and work together on common goals

This is why the three Rs are of such great value when working with groups: they give people a language to organize their thoughts and work together on common goals.

TRY THIS: SPOT THE THREE RS

Sit in on a meeting and make a note of what people say. Organize what has been said into three categories:

- A statement of reality or a question about reality – how things are or how we think they are

- A statement of results or a question about results – how we want things to be or what we want to achieve

- A statement of a response or a question about a response – what we will do or what action needs to be taken

Is the conversation well balanced or is one of these three elements missing?

We were once asked to help a group of politicians who wanted to come up with a strategy for improving school performance in a major city. The schools in that city had been near the bottom of the league tables for a long time. Everyone knew that there was a problem and something needed to be done about it. The difficulty was that the different politicians disagreed on what the problem was, and so had failed to agree on a coherent plan.

One of them thought that the problem was that fewer than 30 percent of the children were achieving the expected grades, way below the national average at the time (*reality*). Another wanted all children to leave school with the skills required for the type of jobs that would be around in the future (*result*). Yet another was convinced that what was most important was to recruit high-quality head teachers in all the schools (*response*). We used the three Rs to help them organize their thoughts and they could immediately see that rather than disagreeing, they were merely focusing on different parts of the same story. They told us later that they had made more progress in that one meeting than in the previous six years.

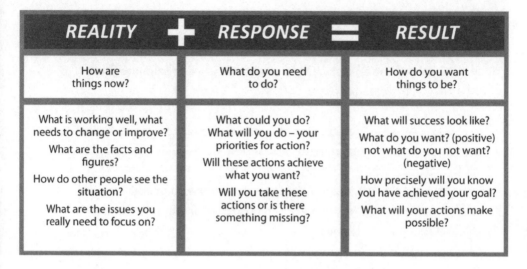

REALITY +	RESPONSE =	RESULT
How are things now?	What do you need to do?	How do you want things to be?
What is working well, what needs to change or improve? What are the facts and figures? How do other people see the situation? What are the issues you really need to focus on?	What could you do? What will you do – your priorities for action? Will these actions achieve what you want? Will you take these actions or is there something missing?	What will success look like? What do you want? (positive) not what do you not want? (negative) How precisely will you know you have achieved your goal? What will your actions make possible?

Figure 17   Using the three Rs

One practical way to use the three Rs to organize your thoughts is with three sheets of paper. Lay the three sheets out as shown in Figure 17 and head the first sheet Reality, the middle one Response, and the final one Result. Think about a breakthrough you want to make and whatever thoughts come up, write them down on Post-it® notes or index cards. Then organize them on the appropriate sheet. You will probably find that you have given much more attention to one of the three Rs than to the other two. The figure gives some ideas for other questions you can ask yourself that can flesh out your thinking.

The most common confusion when using the three Rs is between response and results. It is easy to have an idea such as "I need to improve communication in the team" when the real goal is something bigger, such as "I want the team to work together well toward common goals." Improving communication is a means, not an end. The questions to ask to end the confusion are: "What will that make possible for us?" or "What will that achieve for us?"

The other confusion is between reality and response. The thought "we need to improve communication" is really a suggested response to some aspect of the reality. The reality may be something like "communication is poor," which is very vague, or it could be "members of the team don't keep each other informed," which is more specific. The question to ask here is: "Can I give an example, some experience or incident that illustrates what I mean?"

In general, the use of precise language, as discussed in Chapter 5, helps to root out vague generalizations and can be used across all of the three Rs. For example, you might ask: "Which members of the team don't keep each other informed?" or "Informed about what, precisely?" Filling in the blanks like this yields a great deal of information and provides a solid foundation to work from.

TURNING KNOW-HOW INTO DO-HOW

The dialogue below illustrates how powerful the three Rs can be in helping to find a way forward, and also shows how the do-how map can be used to help turn know-how into do-how. Matt is in his late 20s and is regarded as a rising star in the property business where he works. When we met him he had recently been pulled out of one of the operational divisions of the business to act as assistant to the managing director. Matt asked Dave to help him identify some development goals. He was eager to make a breakthrough in his career, but had no idea what to do to move forward. Dave uses the three Rs to help Matt organize his thoughts. Initially his attention was placed almost entirely on his problems (*reality*), with some thought given to what he might do (*response*). He had paid very little attention to what he wanted (*result*). Later in the conversation, Dave uses the do-how map to help Matt spot his hidden rules.

Dave: What's the breakthrough you want to make?
Matt: I've been given this new job working alongside Bill (the managing director) and I know I should feel grateful for the opportunity to rub shoulders with the board, but I'm not sure where it's leading. I feel like his PA. (*reality*)
Dave: Where do you want it to lead? (*result*)
Matt: I just need experience. I spend most of my time doing photocopying or preparing papers for Bill's meetings. I want to get the most out of this opportunity, but I don't feel that I'm learning what I need to learn. (*reality*)

Dave: What do you want to get out of the opportunity? (*result*)

Matt: I'm not sure. I don't know how I'm seen by Bill and the other directors. I haven't heard of anyone else being asked to take on this role. I'm not sure what Bill wants for me. (*reality*) I need to talk to Bill. (*response*)

Dave: What do you want to get out of your conversation with Bill? (*result*)

Matt: It's my career. I don't want to get stuck as some glorified PA. (*negative result*)

Dave: So what *do* you want?

Matt: I'd like to see myself in a senior management position in ten years or so. (*result*) I think I've got the capability if I can get the experience. (*reality*) I need to learn more about finance and project management, though. (*response*)

Dave: So you want to end up in senior management? (*result*)

Matt: Yes, but I need to learn more. (*response*)

Dave: What would you need to be learning about to feel like you were progressing toward a senior management post? (*response*)

Matt: Some of my peers at the depot where I was based before are getting trained in project management. I've always had a talent for projects, but I've had no formal training. I feel like I'm missing out. (*reality*)

Dave: And what does Bill think? (*reality*)

Matt: I've no idea, I haven't asked him. (*reality*)

Dave: Could you do that? (*response*)

Matt: I'm not sure. I don't want to appear ungrateful for this opportunity and I don't want to look like I haven't thought things through for myself. (*hidden rule*)

Dave: Do you feel uncomfortable about discussing these issues with Bill? (*do-how moment*)

Matt: Yes, I do a bit. I don't want to be pushy. (*hidden rule*) I've talked this over endlessly with my girlfriend and she thinks I need to say something, but somehow there never seems to be a right moment. (*reality*)

Dave: But you do want to keep your career development on track? (*result*)

Matt: Yes, but what if he thinks I'm criticizing him? It might come across wrong. I'm not sure where to start with this. I don't know what Bill wants. I keep on going around in circles in my head and I don't see a way forward. I know I need to raise the issue with Bill, but I'm not sure how to do it. (*unable to visualize the breakthrough*)

Dave: Let's see where we've got to. It sounds to me that you want to end up in senior management (*result*) and that you aren't clear how what you're doing now is going to help you achieve that goal. You feel like a glorified PA. (*reality*) What you need is a clear plan for your career development and the person you need to talk that over with is Bill. More specifically, you would like to get some training in project management. (*response*) [Dave summarizes the outcome Matt wants, his situation, and what he needs to do using the three Rs]

Matt: When you summarize it like that it sounds so straightforward. I'd also like to get involved in some projects. There are many things I could do for Bill if he would let me. (*response*)

Dave: Or if you asked? (*suggested breakthrough behavior*)

THE DO-HOW MAP

At this point, Matt knows what he needs to do. He knew what he needed to do before he even spoke to Dave, in fact, but he didn't do it. He felt stuck, going around in circles, analyzing the situation in his mind. The do-how map is what helps Matt choose the upward fork. From this point on, Dave uses the do-how map to help Matt turn his know-how into do-how.

Matt: I've tried to ask, but the right occasion never seems to come. I assume he had a reason for putting me in this role. I'm surprised that Bill hasn't brought this up. (*subtle blame, which potentially leaves Matt feeling powerless*)

Dave: But he hasn't, so what can you do? (*encouraging responsibility*)

Matt: I suppose I'm just going to have to summon up the courage. (*starting to take responsibility and identify a breakthrough*)

Dave: What would it be like if you did have the courage? (*picturing the breakthrough*)

Matt: I'd have a conversation with Bill like we are having now. But I don't know how Bill will respond. (*hidden rules*)

Dave: Would it help to practice how you would raise the issue with Bill? (*practicing will help Matt visualize the breakthrough*)

Matt: Yes, I think it would.

Dave: Imagine that I'm Bill and tell me what you might say. (*picturing the breakthrough*)

Matt: Bill, I've got a problem with how my role is working out… There, you see how it's going to come across badly! (*hidden rules*: one of Matt's rules is to focus on problems)

Dave: You started with the problem. Sometimes people feel uncomfortable asking for what they want. Is that how you feel? (*pointing out the do-how moment*)

Matt: Yes, I've had that feedback before. It just feels pushy. (*more specific do-how moment*)

Dave: Tell me a little more about what goes on when you think about asking Bill for what you want. (*uncovering Matt's hidden rules*)

Matt: I imagine it will all go wrong. I get anxious. I know I need to have this conversation, but I keep going around in circles in my head.

Dave: Let me see if I can sum up what you've told me. (*draws Matt's do-how map*)

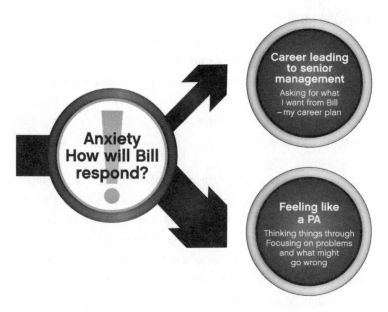

Figure 18   Matt's do-how map

Dave: You feel anxious because you are trying to think through how Bill will respond. You are focusing on the problems and what might go wrong. When you feel like that, you have a choice. You can ask for what you want and just see what happens, letting Bill respond how he will. Let's try again. Try starting with what you want. Start by saying that you see yourself in senior management in the future and you want to talk over how you can get the best out of this assignment. (*modeling the breakthrough behavior*)

Matt: Doesn't that sound cocky? What if Bill doesn't see me that way? I'm doing it again, aren't I? Focusing on what might go wrong, I mean. (*spotting hidden rules*)

Dave: Yes. I'm sure Bill will tell you what he thinks. It doesn't seem cocky to me. It just sounds like you know what you want from your career. Shall we try again?

Matt: Bill, I'd like to talk over how I get the most out of my role. I want to get a clear plan for my career development. I was wondering about some training in project management. Could we talk this over? (*models the breakthrough behavior*)

Dave: That was much better. How did that feel?

Matt: Not too bad. I still find the idea of having this conversation with Bill a bit daunting. (*do-how moment*)

Dave: When you notice that emotion it's a signpost to the choice you have. You can choose to behave the way you normally would, or you can try a different way and see what happens. The main thing is to focus on what you want and listen to what Bill has to say. He will soon tell you if he sees things differently. That would be my advice, but what advice would you like to give yourself when you're in that meeting with Bill? (*inviting positive self-talk*)

Matt: It would be something like "What I want matters."

Dave: Try saying that to yourself before the meeting. Do you think you could have a crack at that?

Matt: Yes.

Dave: Let me know how it goes and don't be afraid to call me if you want to talk anything over.

Dave bumped into Bill on the way out of the building later that day. Bill knew that Dave and Matt had met and told him, "Matt is one the best prospects I've seen in years. I want to make sure we get the best out of him."

Matt rang Dave the following week to report on his meeting with Bill. He was overjoyed at the result. Bill had been delighted to have the opportunity to talk over his career development and had asked him to become involved in a couple of challenging business development projects. He had also agreed about the idea of getting some formal project management training. Matt reported that he felt a weight had been lifted from his shoulders and that he had made a real breakthrough. He told us he had started to notice just how much he focused on problems and had made some other small breakthroughs as a result.

The breakthrough for Matt comes from recognizing that he focuses on problems. He starts the conversation almost entirely consumed with the negative aspects of his situation. When he imagines himself talking to Bill, he pictures talking about his problems and he worries that Bill will respond negatively. The challenge for him is that he's trying to think everything through on his own and he finds it very difficult to ask for what he wants. He plays the situation through in his mind, trying to second-guess how Bill will respond, but he doesn't have the conversation he needs to have. The one thing that can help him move forward is to ask for what he wants, then listen to Bill's response. But when he thinks about talking to Bill, he gets sidetracked into worrying about what Bill will think.

Matt's strengths are his intellectual ability, his attention to detail, and a certain endearing humility that means he is a safe pair of hands and people like working with him. These behaviors have served him well, until faced with a situation where he needs to speak up for himself. Up to this point in his career his ability to think problems through has been an asset. Now he finds himself in a situation where he can't make progress and he feels stuck. Matt is a high flyer with incredible capability, tenacity, and commitment to success. He feels stuck because the very strengths that have got him to where he is now can't help in this situation. He uses the do-how map to spell out the breakthrough he wants, uncover his hidden rules, and recognize that he is at a do-how moment when his choices really do make a difference.

THE DO-HOW MOMENT

What we choose to do at a do-how moment either perpetuates the existing situation or takes us beyond the limits of our hidden rules to create change and deliver results. Whenever you experience a difficult or uncomfortable emotion and you aren't getting the results you want, that is your do-how moment. By understanding and owning your emotional reactions to situations and, rather than fighting them off, recognizing them as the signpost that says "Look here for an opportunity for a breakthrough," you can open up the fork in the road between doing what doesn't work and doing what works. For Matt, this means seeing that his anxiety is not something to be resisted through thinking harder, but is a signal that he is bumping up against the limits he has placed on himself, and that he has the opportunity to let go of his need to think everything through and choose a different approach.

HIDDEN RULES

It's difficult to let go of something that you don't know you're holding on to. But once you spot your habitual patterns of thought and behavior, they can't keep their grip on you. These thoughts are the source of your strengths, but also the source of your limitations. By letting go of what is limiting you in those moments, you can continue to grow and realize your potential. The more familiar you are with your hidden rules, the easier it is to let go of them when they start to limit you. They become useful thoughts rather than absolute truths.

We can see Matt's hidden rules at play during the conversation and how they limit him:

➠ **Intention** – "Avoid problems." Matt has an unconscious intention to avoid things going wrong. This is a negative intention and it's holding him back. That is why the idea of raising his needs with Bill is so uncomfortable. He finds it difficult to ask for what he wants because he expects a negative response. His approach won't work in this situation and he needs to make clear what he needs from Bill.

➠ **Awareness** – "What's the problem, what could go wrong?" Matt is tuned in to notice problems and what could go wrong. It never occurs to him that things might go right. Again, this has served him well, as he has proved to be someone who can be relied on to think things through. In these circumstances this behavior means that he avoids a difficult but necessary conversation with Bill.

⇒ **Action** – "Think things through." Matt's habitual response to any situation is to think through the problems for himself. He can be relied on to take responsibility and come up with a solution to any problem, rather than turning to his manager all the time. This has been one of his greatest strengths, but he is unable to second-guess what Bill has in mind and he needs to talk to Bill.

SPELLING OUT THE BREAKTHROUGH

You've had a lifetime to practice what isn't working in that do-how moment. The road to remaining stuck is broad and well lit, but you can give yourself a better chance of success by creating a clear choice. You do this by spelling out the behavior you want as boldly and vividly as possible.

Making a breakthrough is an act of imagination. The more vividly you can bring the breakthrough you want to life, the more chance you have of making the choices when they arrive. You can use the "four Ps" to picture the positive, precise possibility for the breakthrough you want.

> Once you spot your habitual patterns of thought and behavior, they can't hold on to you

By being clear about what change in behavior you intend to make, you can make it easier to step beyond the limits of your hidden rules.

For Matt, this means being crystal clear about how to state what he wants from Bill in a positive way. By practicing the conversation he wants to have with Bill, he starts to bring it to life. He now knows what this looks like and he also spots how he gets sidetracked into his habitual patterns of focusing on problems, so he can clearly see the choice he has to make.

TAKE RESPONSIBILITY FOR YOUR CHOICES

Even if you recognize that you have a choice, and even if you know what that choice looks like, you still have to make that decision. This isn't easy. The emotions you experience drive you down the lower fork toward your habitual behavior. Choosing the breakthrough rather than acting out of your emotional need requires courage. Practicing the breakthrough behavior makes the upper fork larger and more accessible. The more you practice, the easier it will be for you to choose that behavior when you want to or need to.

You can sabotage your own success by blaming other people or events for the problems and difficulties you face, in the same way that Matt wanted to blame Bill for his discomfort. This attitude can leave you feeling powerless and thinking that there is nothing you can do. By recognizing that the roots of your discomfort always come from within and asking "What can I do?" you can transform feelings of powerlessness into the capacity to take responsibility and turn any adversity into a source of advantage. For Matt, this means taking responsibility for raising his concerns and difficulties rather than blaming the company or Bill for the situation.

OUR HABITS DON'T GIVE UP WITHOUT A FIGHT

In the past, the hunters of West Africa had an ingenious technique for catching monkeys. They would take a heavy cage into the jungle and inside it place a large fruit such as a pineapple. The cage was such that the monkey could put its hand between the bars, but the pineapple could not pass through them. The hunter would hide in the bushes and wait for the monkey. The monkey would arrive and slip its hand between the bars to grasp the pineapple. The hunter would appear, but rather than flee the scene, the monkey would grip ever tighter onto its prize, not wanting to give it up. The monkey would be so attached to the idea of a delicious pineapple that he would fail to let go. The hunter would catch the monkey, roast it, and eat it!

Hopefully, that fate won't befall us, but sometimes it is like this with our habits. We are so attached to them that we can't let go, and we are roasted by our emotions as a result.

Howard, the managing director of an office supplies company, had achieved much in his life. He had always been a natural leader and

203

fighter for what he believed in. He was never scared to take on a challenge. We worked alongside Howard to turn around a failing organization, and saw at first hand how he gave the management team self-belief and confidence while they had seen themselves as failures. This was done against the odds, with talk of a hostile takeover in the air. Howard had to use all his guts and determination to turn things around. During this process, he learned the value of moderating his normally directive style and listening more carefully to his management team before making the big decisions. His fighting spirit was directed outward, toward the hostile forces waiting to move in. This built an atmosphere of trust and camaraderie among the team.

The one problem Howard was left with was that he didn't have someone by his side as a deputy who had the necessary experience. The ideal person was an old colleague, so Howard decided to recruit him. The management team got wind of his plan and were both hurt and angry by what he was now doing. There was a great danger that he would undo nearly 18 months of hard work and divide the team. A small delegation was sent to express the concerns of the team to Howard. Why couldn't he promote someone from inside the organization? Howard was angry at his authority being questioned and privately told us, "I'll take the lot of them on, and I'll win!" Having won the real battle, his fighting spirit was now looking for the next challenge.

Fortunately, he had the courage to take a long, hard look in the mirror, and after some encouragement he stepped back from his defiant stand and started to listen. He listened to his team, but he also listened to his own concerns that were driving his behavior. He didn't compromise, he still recruited from outside, but he did so out of freedom, rather than out of habit. He narrowly avoided an emotional roasting from the flames of his own anger.

Howard had started to face up to his natural inclination to stand and fight, whatever challenged him. During the process of coming to terms with his habitual behavior, he spotted just how vulnerable he felt. This was his do-how moment. The feeling of being vulnerable was what drove the fighting spirit. These were uncomfortable times for Howard. His whole life, his demeanor, even his stature said to the world, "I'm invincible, don't mess with me." But while this air of invincibility had led to much success, it had isolated him from many around him. The real breakthrough came when he found the humility to admit to his team that he needed to bring in someone from outside because he felt isolated and vulnerable. If you can grasp the habit-shattering weight of that admission, you'll realize why Howard is on his way from know-how to do-how, and from being a good leader to being a great leader.

If you follow the simple steps we have outlined in this book with courage and tenacity, you will make a breakthrough. Start with what irks you or is difficult or anything you aren't happy about, and have the courage to acknowledge it. Organize your thoughts using the three Rs to map out your change journey from where you are to where you want to be and how you will get there. Then use the do-how map to get to grips with how you get in the way of your own success. All it takes is honesty with yourself and the commitment to apply a few simple principles. If you take these steps with respect to the challenges in your life and your work, there really is nothing standing in the way of your success. Change may be difficult, but it's always possible.

There really is nothing standing in the way of your success

TRY THIS: YOUR DO-HOW MAP

Think of a breakthrough that you want to make. Draw your do-how map.

What is your do-how moment? What is the situation where your choice of behavior can make a significant impact? What emotion do you experience? What thoughts do you have?

What are your hidden rules? What do you habitually do? What are you holding onto that is limiting you?

What is the breakthrough? Can you picture it? Is it positive and precise? Is it what you really want or are you acting out of impossibility?

What changes will you make to your ways of behaving and thinking? Have you taken responsibility for change by letting go of the limiting idea that it's somebody else who needs to change?

Find an opportunity to practice.

Chapter 10

FROM DO-HOW TO DO-NOW
What future will you
make possible?

When you apply everything we have covered in this book, one of the first things you will notice is how quickly you achieve a breakthrough. Most people can make progress rapidly. The more you practice with the do-how map, the more you will get out of it. You will have insights into how you think and how others think. You will start to overcome the habitual patterns of intention, awareness, and action that get in the way of you achieving your goals. What seemed impossible a few months ago may now seem straightforward. You will discover that you can move forward on challenges you have been stuck on for months or even years. What would have taken hours of conversation now seems to happen in only a few minutes. If you take the time to understand and apply the simple steps we have described, you will be able to put the do-how map into practice and make what now seems impossible appear practical and doable in your work and life. Figure 19 summarizes the key steps and some of the tools and techniques.

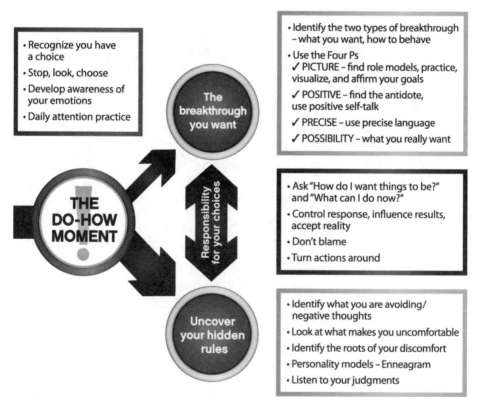

Figure 19   Making the do-how map work for you

We can't say which parts will be most helpful to you. For some people, merely the idea that they have a choice is enough to precipitate a breakthrough. For others, change is more like churning butter: it takes long, hard work, crafting detailed goals and developing self-awareness. We have even met old clients who told us that at the time what we had to say didn't make much impact, but then something suddenly clicked and they made a breakthrough where they hadn't thought one was possible.

FROM NOUGHT TO ONE

Monty Roberts, the great horse trainer, says that if you see learning as a journey from nought to ten, then what is most important is to get from nought to one. In other words, if you can get started then you will tend to complete the rest of the journey. Sometimes when you are stuck it can feel like a breakthrough if you are able to take a small step forward. Identifying what that step looks like can be energizing as you realize the possibility of success. The nought to one in this context is to start practicing with the do-how map.

If you have followed the exercises we have suggested, you will have made a start and you will have learned a great deal. You may even have made a breakthrough with some challenge of your own. You will also have lots of questions about how you can make the do-how map work for you. The most important questions, we find, are the ones about how to put what you have learned into practice.

If you really want to learn how to use the do-how map, you have to *use* it. The cycle that leads to breakthroughs is *idea* leads to *practice* leads to *insight* leads to a *breakthrough*. You start with an idea presented in these pages, but as you practice you will gain insights and start to develop your own experience about how you can use the approach to make further breakthroughs. When employed systematically and with conviction, the approaches we have set out work reliably.

When we work with clients or run development programs, we always ask people to do something practical between sessions. That's when the learning starts, when they confront their own reactions to a different way of doing things. With that new information comes the opportunity to discern what is working and where they are still stuck. It's easy to see who has genuinely had a go at something new from the questions they ask. The people who have tried something practical tend to have practical questions about how to apply what they have learned. They also have insights that allow them to ask questions that might not seem obvious.

There are a million theoretical questions that you could ask and we could answer, but it's very unlikely that they would make any difference on their own and nothing would change. But when you *do* something new, when you try to *apply* what you have learned, even if it's clumsily and unskillfully, that's when the learning begins and that's when the seeds of change are planted. You will find new ways of applying what we have shared, ways that work for you and your situation.

That's the difference between know-how and do-how. When you learn new information you might have some interesting ideas or concepts, but you don't have any insights of your own. Nothing inside you has been challenged or changed. It's when you take those ideas and put them into practice that you really learn something new.

Imagine that you have never swung a golf club. You could read everything there is about golf and you would have a head full of ideas, but you wouldn't have really learned anything. However, when you finally pick up a golf club and swing it at the ball, you find out a lot. Even if you miss the ball, you have still learned a great deal. We are not saying that everything you have read is a waste of time, simply that it doesn't have any real meaning until you have some experiences to learn from.

It's the same with any of the practical skills we take for granted in the workplace. For example, suppose you want to understand why people keep banging on about the importance of giving positive feedback. (And we do bang on about this to our clients.) You may have read about this or learned something on a training program. But all the know-how in the world won't make any difference until you turn it into do-how. The only way you are going to get an insight into why people feel so passionately about this is by taking the time to give those around you some positive feedback and looking at what you discover. When you do this you will learn a great deal. You may learn that you don't know how to give people positive feedback, which is useful to be aware of. Or you could learn that you feel uncomfortable, which is an insight that could point to a do-how moment and an opportunity for a breakthrough. You might just learn how good it feels to give people something that costs you nothing but makes them feel like a million dollars.

> **All the know-how in the world won't make any difference until you turn it into do-how**

DON'T TRY, DO

We were discussing the ideas in this book with an old friend, Rob. He has a way with words and we asked him how he would sum up the key message we wanted to get across. With a cheeky grin, he crouched down and in his best imitation of Yoda from *Star Wars* said, "Do or do not, there is no try." Rob certainly captured something essential about what we have been saying. Over the years we have come to realize that when people tell us that they tried something, it often means that they thought about it but didn't take any meaningful action. Lurking behind "trying" is often the thought "there is nothing I can do" or "this won't make any difference." Trying can also mean going through the motions, but without any conviction or belief. The outer form is there but not the inner thought processes. This matters. Breakthroughs come when we choose to act and think in a way that is consistent with the results we want. At best, trying is the acting without the thinking. At worst, it is giving up before we have even started.

For example, people who listen well don't *try* to listen; they do whatever it takes to understand another person's world. When one approach doesn't work they adapt. They have their eyes (and ears) firmly fixed on the goal. Their thoughts are about how they can listen. Their actions radiate "Your views matter to me" and their words say "I want to understand you." There's no trying in that, just doing.

We are not suggesting that you will get the result you want first time around. Remember, you can't control your outcomes. What you can control is the choices you make about what you think, say, and do.

The only failure is a failure to learn from your experiences

Sometimes people genuinely have a go at a new approach but become disheartened when their first attempt is rebuffed. Don't give up at this point. There will be something you can learn. The only failure is a failure to learn from your experiences.

For any action there will be a result. We can never be sure what will work and what will flop. Some actions will work, others won't. When we step outside the comfort zone of our habitual behavior, there will always be the temptation to give up at the first sign of failure. Our hidden rules want to reassert themselves and guide us back within the limits they have set. Each time we try something new, we can see it as an iteration that moves us closer to discovering what works. In this way we can improve our response so that we move nearer to getting the result we want. What is important is to recognize any discomfort that arises for what it is, a signpost to a breakthrough, and ask ourselves what we will do differently next time.

WHAT'S YOUR GROUNDHOG DAY?

Let's return to Bill Murray and *Groundhog Day*, which we mentioned in Chapter 2. Bill's character, Phil, relives the same day over and over again. This provides him with the opportunity to try a new approach each day until he finally gets what he wants, Rita, played by Andie McDowell. Not only that, Phil himself is changed by his experiences.

You might think that this is a fantasy film and nothing like this happens in real life. We don't agree. In our experience, the areas where people get stuck repeat themselves over and over again. Haven't you ever sat in a meeting at work and felt like you are going around the same conversations, or met an old friend and realized that they are complaining about the same things they complained about five years ago? What have you got so used to being dissatisfied with that you have forgotten you have the power to change it? We can complain about our circumstances as much as we want, but until we learn, as Phil did, that each new day is a fresh opportunity to try something new and get a different result, we will remain stuck.

Whatever your experience of life and work, you are a co-creator, not a spectator. The roots of your future are not in the way things are or the circumstances you find yourself in, they are in the choices you make. For any breakthrough you want to make, there is a way of thinking and behaving that can deliver that breakthrough. The price of personal growth is that you are willing to let go of what is holding you back. When you see that, you will find that you have the freedom to choose. You can let go of the way things have been and choose how they will become.

You are a co-creator, not a spectator

So what has your Groundhog Day been like? What are the patterns that repeat in your life and work that you want to change? What future will you make possible when you know that anything is possible?

TRY THIS: WHAT DID YOU DO AND WHAT DID YOU LEARN?
Having been through the various exercises, discovered about the different aspects of the do-how map, and, hopefully, tried some new approaches, take some time to review what you have learned.

What did you notice about the emotions and thoughts that are triggered as you experience a do-how moment?

When can your choices make the most difference?

Are you clear about the breakthrough you want
to make? Can you visualize it? Do you have a role
model for how you want to behave?

What insights have you had about what you
habitually think and do? What hidden rules have you
spotted?

What different choices have you made about your
behavior? What has the result of these choices
been?

What else did you learn from what you did or tried?

RECOMMENDED READING
AND RESOURCES

Over the years, our thinking has been strongly influenced by various people we have met and books we have read. There are so many great books that we can't list every one that has helped us, but below are a small selection of works that we have found valuable.

Robert Anthony (2004) *Beyond Positive Thinking: A No-Nonsense Formula for Getting the Results You Want*, Morgan James Publishing. Illustrates the importance of visualization and positive thinking.

Renée Baron & Elizabeth Wagele (1994) *The Enneagram Made Easy: Discover the 9 Types of People*, Thorsons. Another great book on the enneagram, with very helpful illustrations.

Meredith R. Belbin (2010) *Team Roles at Work*, Butterworth Heinemann. A fascinating read and useful when working with teams.

Isabel Briggs Myers & Peter B. Myers (1995) *Gifts Differing: Understanding Personality Type*, Davies Black/Nicholas Brealey Publishing. The most widely used personality typing approach.

Marcus Buckingham & Donald O. Clifton (2005) *Now, Discover Your Strengths: How to Develop Your Talents and Those of the People You Manage*, Pocket Books. The strengths-based approach is a good way to start learning about hidden rules.

Charles Duhigg (2012) *The Power of Habit: Why We Do What We Do, and How to Change*, William Heinemann. A good overview of the power that habits have over our life and work.

Viktor E. Frankl (1959) *Man's Search for Meaning: The Classic Tribute to Hope from the Holocaust*, Washington Square Press. An inspiring book about personal responsibility.

Marshall Goldsmith (2008) *What Got You Here Won't Get You There: How Successful People Become Even More Successful*, Profile Books. A useful overview of how every strength eventually becomes a limitation.

Daniel Goleman (1996) *Emotional Intelligence: Why It Can Matter More Than IQ*, Bloomsbury. A classic must-read for anyone who wants to understand the importance of emotions and emotional intelligence.

Tracy Goss (1996) *The Last Word on Power*, Piatkus. Illustrates the importance of language in what we achieve, and a book that made a big impact on us.

John Grinder & Richard Bandler (1989) *The Structure of Magic: A Book About Language and Therapy*, vos 1 and 2, Science and Behavior Books. From the creators of NLP, these two books tell you everything you need to know about the importance of precise language. Not an easy read but well worth the effort.

Byron Katie & Stephen Mitchell (2002) *Loving What Is: How Four Questions Can Change Your Life*, Rider. Probably the best book there is on turning around actions and taking responsibility.

Robert Kegan & Lisa Lahey (2009) *Immunity to Change: How to Overcome It and Unlock the Potential in Yourself and Your Organization*, Harvard Business School Press. Illustrates how existing ways of thinking get in the way of change.

John P. Kotter (1996) *Leading Change*, Harvard Business School Press. Kotter is an acknowledged expert on organizational change and his books are packed full of useful insights and case studies.

Ginger Lapid-Bogda (2009) *Bringing Out the Best in Everyone You Coach: Use the Enneagram System for Exceptional Results*, McGraw-Hill Professional. A useful book about using the enneagram in the workplace.

Jim Loehr (2008) *The Power of Story: Change Your Story, Change Your Destiny in Business and in Life*, Free Press. Full of great examples of how our personal narrative determines the results we get.

Dan P. McAdams (1997) *The Stories We Live By: Personal Myths and the Making of the Self*, Guilford Press. The classic work on the power of personal narrative.

Paul McGee (2004) *S.U.M.O. (Shut Up, Move On): The Straight Talking Guide to Creating and Enjoying a Brilliant Life*, Capstone. A great little book that delivers powerful messages about change in a light-hearted and memorable way.

Thich Nhat Hanh (1991) *The Miracle of Mindfulness*, Rider. The classic work on mindfulness by one of the world's most respected Zen teachers.

Harold Ramis (dir.) (1993) *Groundhog Day*, Columbia Pictures. Regarded by some critics as a masterpiece of 1990s popular cinema, great fun to watch but with an important message about how we can make a breakthrough.

Srikymar Rao (2007) *Are You Ready to Succeed? Unconventional Strategies for Achieving Personal Mastery in Business and in Life*, Rider. Based on Dr. Rao's ever popular course at London and Columbia business schools.

Monty Roberts (2001) *Horse Sense for People*, HarperCollins. Monty Roberts is an extraordinary man and his books contain a great deal of common-sense advice.

Eric Salmon (2003) *The ABC of the Enneagram: Identifying the Different Forces That Energise Us*, Institute for Outdoor Learning. Our favorite book on the enneagram. Sadly out of print, but if you find a copy, buy it.

Martin E.P. Seligman (2007) *What You Can Change and What You Can't: Learning to Accept What You Are*, Nicholas Brealey Publishing. From the founder of the science of positive psychology, a useful guide to what you can change, packed full of helpful insights.

Hal & Sidra Stone (1988) *Embracing Our Selves: Voice Dialogue Manual*, Nataraj Publishing. Offers powerful insights into how our internal narrative shapes our behavior.

Bill Torbert (2004) *Action Inquiry: The Secret of Timely and Transforming Leadership*, Berrett-Koehler. Offers insights into how a change of narrative can lead to a leadership breakthrough.

Andrew Weiss (2004) *Beginning Mindfulness: Learning the Way of Awareness*, New World Libary. Mindfulness has become mainstream in the last few years and there are many great books on the subject, but this is one of the simplest and the best.

Ken Wilber (2000) *Integral Psychology: Consciousness, Spirit, Psychology, Therapy*, Shambala. Ken Wilber's work is like Marmite: you either love it or hate it. We love it, particularly his ideas about personal growth.

Timothy Wilson (2011) *Redirect: The Surprising New Science of Psychological Change*, Allen Lane; and (2002) *Strangers to Ourselves: Discovering the Adaptive Unconscious*, Harvard University Business Press. Reading Timothy Wilson's work helped us understand how small changes in our personal story can have a big impact.

Steve Zaffron & Dave Logan (2011) *The Three Laws of Performance: Rewriting the Future of Your Organization and Your Life*, Jossey Bass. A book that seems to have been inspired by the work of Werner Erhardt.

Rosamund & Ben Zander (2000) *The Art of Possibility: Transforming Professional and Personal Life*, Harvard Business School Press. Shows the importance of thinking from possibility rather than impossibility. Look up Ben Zander on ted.com, he's an inspiration.

TRY THIS: GIVE US YOUR FEEDBACK

We'd love to hear about your experiences and breakthroughs using the do-how map. We hope you will visit the website at www.the-do-how.com and tell us how you have got on. If you have questions, particularly questions about how to put do-how into practice, we'd be delighted to hear them.

FIND OUT MORE

To find out more about how you can apply the ideas in this book for yourself or in your organization, visit:

www.the-do-how.com

ACKNOWLEDGMENTS

We would need many pages to thank everyone who has helped either directly or indirectly in creating this book. Let's start with all those people we have learned from. There are countless people whose insights we have read through their writings. Some of the most important to us are mentioned in the Recommended Reading and we are grateful to them all. Special thanks go to those who made a more personal impact through the lessons we learned directly from them: people like Jim Platts, Tony Marmont, and Thich Nhat Hanh. We are particularly grateful to Jeff Pitt, the best facilitator, trainer, and change agent we ever met, who sadly died at the age of 44. What we learned from Jeff changed how we saw the world and how we worked.

A particularly big thank-you must go to Owen Williams, who is not only a role model for turning know-how into do-how, but is the client who gave us the push we needed to get on and actually write this book. Without Owen we doubt that the book would ever have been written.

Our thanks also go to all those who helped read through the early drafts and gave us useful feedback about how to present our messages. Chief among these is Nick Brealey, who is not only a legendary publisher but a genius who never gave up on us until we really did get our story clear. Thanks also to Andy Rhodes, Michael Hoar, Julian Ward, Andrea Baqai, Vari McLuskie, Beth Corbet, Ruth Corbet, and Cath Corbet, who all read early drafts and helped to shape the final work. A special mention goes to Rob Weston, whose way with words helped us turn raw ideas into something more memorable.

We would like to thank our editors Sally Lansdell and Susannah Lear, who polished some pretty rough diamonds and also offered up a few gems of their own in the process. We extend our gratitude also to all the staff at Nicholas Brealey Publishing who have helped us in countless ways.

A picture is worth a thousand words and on that basis Vicky Bembridge and Gary Love deserve a huge thank-you for turning our scribbled doodles into the crisp and meaningful figures you find in this book.

Finally, we'd like to thank each one of our clients over nearly 20 years in business. Every project we have ever worked on has felt like a privilege and we thank all those people who have seen fit to share their problems and challenges with us. This book has grown out of what we learned together on that journey.

INDEX

A

accepting reality 157–8

actions 125, 190–91, 202

    habitual 36–9, 120

Alan, contract catering company, breakthrough at work 16–17, 21, 49, 51, 52

appreciative inquiry 3

awareness 76–80, 125, 190–91, 201

    capacity for 29

    limited 36–9, 120

B

behavior, choice of 31–3, 45, 51

blame 151–5

    culture 181–2

    relinquishing 153–5

breakthrough 2, 3–5, 6, 15–18, 26, 44, 49–51, 61

    cycle of 209

    desired 53, 55, 83–110

    personal 17–18

    question 192

    spelling out 53, 55, 108–10, 202

    starting point for 188–9

    two kinds of 84–5

C

change programs, failure of 12–13

change

    organizational 5, 13, 165–85

    personal 5, 13

    possibility of 2, 44

trying 211–12

V

visualization 91–2

W

Will, politician, defining goal 84–5, 88, 97–8